MYSELF AGAIN

The PARENTS Postpartum Survival Guide

Gabrielle Mauren, PhD

Michelle Wiersgalla, MD

Praeclarus Press, LLC

www.PraeclarusPress.com

Praeclarus Press, LLC
2504 Sweetgum Lane
Amarillo, Texas 79124 USA
806-367-9950
www.PraeclarusPress.com

DISCLAIMER

The information contained in this publication is advisory only
and is not intended to replace sound clinical judgment or individualized patient care. The author disclaims all warranties,
whether expressed or implied, including any warranty as the
quality, accuracy, safety, or suitability of this information for
any particular purpose.

ISBN: 978-1-946665-52-2

Cover Design: Ken Tackett
Developmental Editing: Kathleen Kendall-Tackett
Copyediting: Chris Tackett
Layout & Design: Nelly Murariu

CONTENTS

Chapter 1
Introduction   **1**

Chapter 2
The PARENTS Method   **7**

P – Practice patience   8

A – Activities for Yourself   9

R – Rest and Sleep   10

E – Exercise or Movement   13

N – Nutrition   13

T – Time with Others   15

S – Support Network   16

Chapter 3
The Baby Blues   **19**

Patient Story - Monica   19

The Baby Blues: The Basics   20

Causes and Contributing Factors   25

Misunderstandings About the Baby Blues   26

PARENTS and the Baby Blues   28

Revisiting Monica   33

Chapter 4
The Edinburgh Postnatal Depression Scale 35

Chapter 5
Depression   43

Patient Story - Alecia   43

Postpartum Depression: The Basics   44

Typical Symptoms of Postpartum Depression   46

Causes and Contributing Factors   53

Patient Story - Denise   56

Misunderstandings About Postpartum

Depression   57

PARENTS and Postpartum Depression   61

Revisiting Alecia   68

Revisiting Denise   70

Chapter 6
Postpartum Depression in
Their Own Words   71

Alecia   72

Denise   77

Chapter 7
Anxiety   **85**

Patient Story - Krystal   85

Postpartum Anxiety: The Basics   86

Typical Symptoms of Postpartum Anxiety   87

Postpartum Panic Attacks   90

Patient Story - Jaclyn   92

Postpartum Obsessive-Compulsive Disorder   93

A Note on "OCD"   97

Causes and Contributing Factors   98

Misunderstandings about Postpartum Anxiety   100

PARENTS and Postpartum Anxiety   103

Revisiting Krystal   111

Revisiting Jaclyn   113

Chapter 8
Antepartum and Postpartum Anxiety
in Their Own Words   **115**

Krystal   115

Jaclyn   120

Chapter 9
Depression and Anxiety in Dads and
Other Parents   125

Patient Story - James   125

Emotional Distress in Non-Birth Parents:
  The Basics   127

Typical Symptoms of Postnatal Depression
  and Anxiety   128

Causes and Contributing Factors   136

Patient Story - Kim   138

Misunderstandings about Postnatal Depression
  and Anxiety   140

PARENTS and Postnatal Depression and
  Anxiety in Non-Birth Parents   142

Revisiting James   147

Revisiting Kim   148

Chapter 10
Traumatic Experiences in Pregnancy
and Childbirth   151

Patient Story - Brianna   151

Pregnancy Trauma and Traumatic
  Childbirth: The Basics   153

Typical Symptoms of Trauma   157

Causes and Contributing Factors   162

Patient Story - Marisol   163

Misunderstandings about Traumatic Childbirth   165

PARENTS and Trauma   168

Revisiting Brianna   173

Revisiting Marisol   175

Chapter 11
The PARENTS Method Worksheet   177

Chapter 12
Treatment Options   181

Medication   183

Misunderstandings about Medication   186

Psychotherapy   189

Misunderstandings about Psychotherapy   195

Involving Loved Ones in Appointments
  and Decisions   197

Chapter 13
Preparing for Future Pregnancies   199

Chapter 14
Your Postpartum Plan   207

My Postpartum Plan   210

Sample - My Postpartum Plan   214

Chapter 15

Selected Resources 219

Maternal and Parental Mental Health   219

Peer Groups for Moms   221

Lactation Support   222

Other Resources   223

Phone/Tablet Apps   224

References 225

Research on the Safety of Psychiatric Medications

During Pregnancy and Lactation   229

About the Authors 233

CHAPTER 1

INTRODUCTION

We are so glad that you found this book! We hope that you find the information in these pages informative, reassuring, and helpful. We decided to write this book to help new parents manage the changes that come with having a new baby, especially those who may encounter mental health challenges during this time of transition. This information and advice are for those who are parents for the first time, the second, or more, and for future parents who want to be prepared for anything.

We have worked as clinicians and educators in the field of reproductive psychiatry and psychology for a combined 20+ years. The patients we care for are usually pregnant, postpartum, or planning a pregnancy. As part of our work, we collaborate closely with obstetricians, primary care doctors, midwives, nurses, lactation consultants, doulas, and others who care for these parents and future parents. For example, the midwives in our healthcare system organize their prenatal care appointments into group sessions called "Centering Pregnancy," rather than individual clinic appointments, which allows for a shared experience among parents-to-be and an efficient means of providing information and education about all things childbirth-related. There are usually 10 group sessions for each cohort of parents, and one of the 10 sessions is focused on the postpartum experience.

We have been invited to speak at these Centering Pregnancy groups many times. We enjoy these sessions because it allows us to share our experience and advice directly with these families. The midwives tell us repeatedly that their patients appreciate our information and insights, and they often say that our session was one of the most helpful in the series. After we left one such session, the two of us looked at each other and had the same thought simultaneously; we should write a book so that we can share this with an even wider audience.

We wrote this book with all types of families in mind, and it is intended for all types of parents – straight, lesbian, gay, cis, trans, non-binary, married, remarried, single, younger, older, etc. We want this book to be useful to people planning pregnancy, expecting a child, or already parenting. Throughout this book, we use inclusive language like "parents" and "parenthood." On some occasions, we use female pronouns, "mom," and "mother." We acknowledge and celebrate that pregnant people and parents come in all varieties, and we intend to include all people in these important conversations about mental health during pregnancy and postpartum.

Thanks to our experience in the worlds of psychiatry and psychology, we can teach about the science and research behind these topics, and thanks to our many and varied audiences, we have learned to give straightforward, simple advice about what to expect during this phase of life. We offer this book as a guide, in plain language, for those who want to understand more about the emotional challenges that can often present themselves after a new baby joins a family. We include essential information about mental health concerns new parents face and practical, realistic advice about how to manage when things get difficult. We provide real-life examples about how symptoms and solutions can look so that those who are strug-gling may see themselves in these scenarios and understand they are not alone. Parenting is usually a delightful experience, but it can also be exhausting, frustrating, and anxiety-provoking. We write about ways to get through the hard parts so that you can enjoy the wonderful parts of forming a family.

It can feel isolating to experience mental health concerns during this time since the message we often hear in Western society is that caring for a baby is endlessly blissful. These messages imply that "you're doing it wrong" if you don't find every moment wonderful. We know, from years of experience and seeing thousands of patients, that people who struggle during or after pregnancy are not alone in that struggle. We hope that this book helps the reader recognize they are not alone or abnormal, and they are not doing it wrong. On the contrary, they're human and living through one of the greatest transitions that life has to offer. Most importantly, there are ways to feel better and to even enjoy parenthood. Although this can be a difficult and sometimes sobering topic, we intend this book to be entertaining, easy to read, and above all, *useful* for new parents and those who love and support them.

You can read this book from cover to cover, but we've also intentionally divided it into easy-to-find sections and subsections. We want busy, tired parents to be able to read on the fly, between all those diaper changes and midnight feedings, about things relevant to them. First, we review our strategies for self-care and stress reduction, using a method we created called "PARENTS." We then cover specific types of symptoms and diagnoses, and apply the PARENTS strategies to illustrate how these approaches can look in real life. We also address the experiences and mental health concerns of non-birth parents, including dads, same-gender partners, and adoptive parents. We review clinical treatment options, including psychotherapies, medications, and other approaches. Finally, we discuss planning for a first pregnancy/postpartum experience or a subsequent one.

In each chapter, you will read about people who have experienced mental health concerns during pregnancy or postpartum. Some stories are summaries of a single person's experience (names and details have been changed to maintain privacy) and others are an amalgamation of the types of people we've worked with to illustrate common experiences. In addition to our case examples, you'll also hear directly from some of these patients in their own writings about their experiences of postpartum depression and anxiety, and what it was like to get treatment.

A note before getting down to business in the rest of this book: it's important for readers to know that this book is not a substitute for professional psychiatric treatment. In each chapter, we discuss when someone should reach out to their healthcare clinician, but readers should not hesitate to ask for professional help at any point, if they are concerned about how they are feeling and functioning. We hope that this book helps readers to confidently manage whatever concerns arise, and most importantly, to enjoy their new families and thrive as parents.

CHAPTER 2

THE PARENTS METHOD

The Importance of Self-Care

One thing that separates parents who thrive from parents who struggle is self-care and stress reduction. There are many approaches to this, and we summarize some of our typical recommendations via the PARENTS method. We provide an overview of these approaches in this chapter and give real-life examples throughout the book of how to employ these strategies.

Though this book is divided into chapters based on the specific mental health concerns parents may experience, we encourage you to review the PARENTS sections in every chapter, as there will be tips, skills, and approaches that may be helpful even if you're not struggling with a particular set of symptoms.

The PARENTS method is illustrated by the following acronym:

P Practice patience

A Activities for yourself

R Rest and sleep

E Exercise or movement

N Nutrition

T Time with others

S Support network

P Practice Patience

Be kind to yourself. No parent can do it all, so let some things slide. If you go to bed some nights with dirty dishes in the sink, but you were able to get some rest, spend some time with your baby or other family members, and do at least one enjoyable activity, consider it a good day. Most parents embark on the journey of having children with high hopes and assumptions about the way things will be once the baby arrives. If those hopes come to pass, that's wonderful. If they don't, but everyone is generally happy and healthy, that's also wonderful. Listen to your heart and your body to get what you need and move whatever you can to the back burner for the first few months with a new baby. Nobody gets parenting exactly right from the outset, and nobody is a perfect parent. Luckily, perfection is not necessary when it comes to raising kids. With some attention to your own needs, you can be a *good* parent, and that's all that families need to thrive.

Activities for Yourself

Stay connected with activities that you enjoy, or used to enjoy, before the baby arrived. When we have an infant, it's easy to lose track of the things that make us who we are because we get lost in diapering, feeding, and getting the baby to sleep. With a newborn, these things can easily consume 24 hours of the day. As parents get into routines, and life with an infant gets more predictable, it can be helpful to reconnect with old hobbies and activities. Before the baby came, did you enjoy running, biking, swimming, or yoga? Were you a card player? Did you relax by binge-watching Netflix? Were you an avid reader? Painter? Musician? Foodie? Did you enjoy going out dancing? Were you active in your place of worship?

It can be challenging to build these activities back into your life, but it's worth the effort. As we often say to our patients, kids do best when their parents feel well. If parents don't have anything that fuels their own happiness, they're less able to be present for their kids and less able to have fun with parenting. When parenting is all we do, all day, every day, it starts to feel burdensome instead of joyful.

Rest and Sleep

When we present this information to audiences, we often start by talking about sleep. There's no doubt that sleep is fantastic, and if you can make it happen, then, by all means, do it. However, it can be unrealistic to build a predictable sleep routine into your schedule when you have an infant. People will often give the advice to "sleep when the baby sleeps" – a great idea if that works for you, but for many people, it just doesn't work. Napping while the sun is out isn't easy for lots of adults, and when the baby sleeps, it's also your opportunity to get other things done like paying bills, folding laundry, and answering work emails. As we worked with more and more parents, we learned that while the ultimate goal might be to get more sleep, the more realistic goal is to get more *rest*. While the baby naps, or while another caregiver takes over, try just sitting in a cozy chair and doing something quiet for a half-hour, or lie down and get comfortable, but if you don't sleep, that's okay. Taking a break from the exhausting work of parenting an infant is a must. In some ways, parenting an infant is like any other job, and in some ways, even more intense and demanding; we wouldn't advise anyone to do any kind of job without taking breaks at least every few hours. Those breaks can keep parents from feeling burned out by the demands of childcare.

In addition to talking about rest, we still talk about nighttime sleep, too. Most adults need at least 7 hours of sleep to function well (Watson et al., 2015). Many people do even better with 8+ hours, but getting by on 6-7 can work, at least temporarily. Like most of the advice we give to our patients, these strategies are intended for parents of infants. As kids get older, these strategies become less necessary because kids become more autonomous and have more consistent routines. The approaches here aren't going to be necessary for the next 18 years, just for the next few months. If you're in a two-parent household, it's important for both parents to aim for around 6 hours of sleep, even if it's not consistent every night. At first, those 6 hours are unlikely to be consecutive. They'll be broken up by the baby waking, but as long as you can cobble together a total of 6 hours, you'll probably do just fine, although advanced calculus may not be an option for your exhausted brain.

We usually advise parents to avoid having one person as the sole nighttime caregiver – this results in one parent being sleep-deprived and one being generally well-rested, and that disparity is not kind to relationship harmony. Lots of couples have made the argument that since one parent is going back to work before the other, the parent who is still at home should get up more often during the night because they have more downtime during the day. That may work for some couples but caring for a newborn can be one of the most taxing and exhausting jobs around and trying to do that job while sleep-deprived is even tougher.

Exercise or Movement

Exercise can be an effective antidepressant and antianxiety strategy (Mayo Clinic, 2021). When most people think of exercise, they think of something like going for a run, being at the gym, or taking an exercise class. These are great options, but with a new baby at home, it can be challenging to find time in your schedule to exercise in this way. Once medically cleared, we encourage all new parents to find time to exercise in whatever form is most enjoyable to you. If you're finding it difficult to get to the gym, we encourage you to think about how you can get more *movement* into your day. This could be a simple walk around the block with the baby in a stroller. You could do jumping jacks or climb your stairs while the baby naps or invite a friend to go to the mall and walk. To get the mood benefits of exercise, you don't need to train for a marathon. You'll gain mental health benefits just from being more physically active in any way.

 Nutrition

The mental health field has relatively recently started to embrace the idea that what we eat can have a significant impact on how we feel.

Lots of research on the mental health benefits of various diets have helped shed light on what may work best. Many authors have written about this topic in ways more detailed than what we'll cover in this book. However, the most common message about healthy eating is that there are no gimmicks or secrets involved – avoid processed foods and excess sugars, try to eat whole foods, mostly vegetables and fruits, lean proteins, and healthy fats. This isn't always the easiest thing to do in American society, and when there's an infant at home, finding time to prepare meals or even to sit down and eat is not always possible.

Planning ahead will simplify things – if you make a few days' worth of meals at a time, this can help cut down on the impulse to grab a less-than-healthy snack just because it's easy. Family and friends may be able to help with meal preparation or sometimes offer to bring meals over for your family – take them up on it. Meal preparation services that deliver ingredients to you can be expensive but may be worth considering as an option for the first few months of your baby's life until routines get established, and you can start to find more time to shop and cook. You don't have to eat a diet of only salmon, kale, and avocados, but if you have the choice between that or things like pizza and sugary sweets, try to choose salmon-kale-avocado, at least some of the time – you'll feel better physically and emotionally.

T Time with Others

Newborns take up a lot of time. It's often surprising to new parents just how much time is involved with caring for a new baby. Recall the days before kids, when friends who had infants would tell you they didn't have time to shower on a particular day. You may have thought to yourself, "how could they not find time to shower when it only takes 10 minutes?" Then you had a newborn of your own, and it seemed a lot more plausible that fitting in a shower just wasn't going to happen some days. Well, if it's hard to carve out those 10 minutes, imagine trying to carve out time to have a date night of a few hours, or to find time to get coffee with a friend, or to fit in any other social activity. Because of that, parents of newborns often find that they feel more and more socially isolated. It's easy to slip into routines at home, and it can be a challenge to get out of the house, or to have guests over.

We encourage our patients to try to prioritize spending time with others. Whether that is a date night or coffee with friends, staying in contact with others can be crucial to feeling well postpartum. Also, while making arrangements for time with a friend or partner is one option, there are other ways to stay social. For example, many places around the country have parent support groups. These may be run by local school districts, healthcare facilities, or private organizations – they can be especially helpful for connecting with other parents who have children the same age so that you can share the joys and struggles of parenthood with people who understand.

S Support Network

We've all heard the saying that it "takes a village" to raise a child. There's a lot of truth to this old adage, but in current society, mass media and social media would imply that a person can work full-time, parent multiple kids, take care of household tasks, maintain great friendships, start a side hustle, lose the baby weight in 2 weeks, and do this all while sporting perfect hair and makeup. Many parents get discouraged because of the expectation that they "do it all." Nobody can do it all because it's simply not possible to be an amazing parent/employee/spouse/friend/son/daughter all the time. There's not enough time in the day to be excellent at every aspect of life – we all need help with some things, sometimes.

Most parents recognize and accept this on some level but may still struggle with asking for help when they need it or even with accepting help when it's offered. You'll do yourself a great service by getting comfortable with asking for, and accepting help; your life will be easier, your load will be lighter, and as a result, you'll be able to enjoy parenting more. It's worthwhile to build your own village to support you and your family. Early on, people may offer to bring meals or come over and help with the baby, and that's great, but don't be shy about asking for more help – you know you've always got a to-do list, so let your friends and family get some of those tasks checked off. They will appreciate feeling like they're important to you, and you know you'd happily volunteer to help if the roles were reversed, so don't hesitate to reach out to them. Once your family is more settled into routines, you won't need to lean on others as much, but in those first several months, accept any and all offers of support.

CHAPTER 3

THE BABY BLUES

For about two weeks after the birth of her first child, Monica found herself feeling more emotional. She would cry at TV commercials and would snap angrily at her husband when he loaded the dishwasher incorrectly. (An aside: Oh, the dishwasher! In our experience, it's a common source of conflict, especially when people are sleep-deprived or not feeling their best. Our inner psychoanalysts would probably say it has something to do with feeling out-of-control and unorganized, which makes a lot of sense since newborns are so unpredictable that they can do an excellent job of making parents feel discombobulated.) This felt not like her at all. She was typically a very level-headed person. After one of these flares of emotion, she would feel better

quickly and be able to recognize that she had overreacted in the situation. Most of the time, she felt like her usual self. But with everything that was new in her life–the baby, staying home from work, having visitors most days, and not sleeping well–she started to wonder if she had postpartum depression.

The Baby Blues: The Basics

Most people have heard of the baby blues. It is a common experience for new mothers. Estimates are that up to 85% of new moms will experience some symptoms of the baby blues (MGH Center for Women's Mental Health, 2021). Many women describe this experience as similar to having premenstrual symptoms (PMS) – having emotional ups and downs, being quick to cry over small concerns, or having moments of irritability. Symptoms typically occur in the first two weeks postpartum. When there is a flare of irritability or an unexpected crying spell, it resolves quickly, and most people feel like they return to their usual self. This is different from postpartum depression or anxiety because, with those, the symptoms don't resolve quickly and can last days, weeks, or even longer. We review those distinctions in more detail in upcoming chapters.

Typical Symptoms of the Baby Blues

The symptoms of the baby blues are common, usually short-lived, and do not get in the way of a person's ability to take care of herself, her children, or her social and occupational tasks. The symptoms of the baby blues include:

» **Moodiness**

Unexpected emotional ups and downs are a hallmark of the baby blues. These rapid emotional shifts—usually sadness or irritability—are fleeting, and there's a quick return to feeling like one's usual self again, often within minutes.

» **Irritability**

Being quick to anger, even over minor annoy-ances, is another common experience. Most women will recognize their irritable reactions as out of proportion to the situation, but they may feel like they couldn't contain their reaction in the moment.

» **Anxiety**

The anxiety some women feel as part of the baby blues is usually rooted in getting adjusted to the transition to parenting. Newborns demand a huge amount of attention – they need your care 24 hours a day. Especially for first-time moms, caring for a new baby can be stressful because it's hard to know what to do and how to make everything go smoothly. For example, it can take several months to learn a baby's different types of cries; in those early weeks, it can be overwhelming trying to figure out what the baby needs, whether she/he is sleeping and eating enough, or how to soothe her/him.

» **Tearfulness**

Being quick to cry is a frequent experience during the baby blues. Mothers tell us they cry unexpectedly over a cute puppy video on social media, after spilling pumped breast milk, or because the store was out of a favorite snack. Typically, there's a quick recovery and return to feeling well again. As with flares of irritability, she can recognize after the fact that her reaction was bigger than the situation called for. Some women also report that tears come when they are feeling overwhelmed: when the newborn is crying, the dog is barking, a mother-in-law is texting, and the doorbell just rang, all at the same time.

» **Trouble sleeping**

Because the baby blues happen in the first two weeks postpartum, most of the sleep problems people face during these early weeks are due to adjusting to interrupted and limited sleep because new babies have so many overnight needs. Feeling exhausted and fatigued is the most common experience when caring for a newborn.

» **Poor concentration**

With attention divided between the new baby, older children, and a multitude of other tasks and all of this in the setting of insufficient sleep, it's not surprising that concentration will be affected. People walk into a room and forget why they went there, they run to the store and forget to buy the one important thing they needed, they forget a close friend's birthday. We've heard lots of examples like these.

Researchers have found evidence that "mommy brain" is real (Glynn & Sandman, 2011; Hoekzema et al., 2017). One theory is that after having a baby, the brain automatically reassigns cognitive resources, with more energy going to the areas of your brain that will allow you to best care for a baby. That may include reassignment of those cognitive resources to things like being able to read emotional cues more effectively. This research suggests that there may be more to "mommy brain" than just being sleep-deprived.

» **Being easily overwhelmed**

Bringing home a new baby is a major life adjustment. It's natural to feel overwhelmed with this responsibility. When it comes to the baby blues, new parents need time to adjust, to learn about their baby's needs and rhythms, and to settle into new day-to-day routines.

When to Reach Out to Your Healthcare Professional

» If you are experiencing many of the symptoms listed above for longer than 2 weeks.

» If, when you experience these symptoms, you don't quickly return to feeling like your typical self. In other words, the feelings aren't short-lived but seem to hang around.

» If these symptoms are not fleeting *and* you notice that they are getting in the way of you doing the things you want and need to do.

» If these symptoms persistently affect your ability to enjoy your life.

» If you are having thoughts of wanting to die or of hurting yourself or someone else. In this situation, you should contact your doctor right away.

Causes and Contributing Factors

There are many things that can contribute to the baby blues. The baby blues probably results from a combination of hormone shifts after delivery, changes in sleep patterns for new parents, and the challenges of adjusting to life with a newborn. Breastfeeding difficulties may trigger symptoms too. All of this is in addition to physically recovering from labor and delivery, from surgery if a mom had a cesarean section, and from any complications that may have arisen during or after delivery. Lack of a good support system can lead to an increased risk of symptoms as well.

The baby blues do not typically require formal treatment. New moms simply need time to rest and heal, to get supports in place, and to get some restful sleep. In most cases, the baby blues resolve on their own by the end of postpartum week two or three.

Misunderstandings About the Baby Blues

» **If I experience the baby blues, I'll probably get postpartum depression.**

The baby blues are experienced in some intensity by almost all moms of newborns in Western cultures, but only about 15% of new moms will develop postpartum depression (Postpartum Support International, 2021). The baby blues appear to be a normal reaction to the causes listed above and don't mean postpartum depression is inevitable. In fact, the majority of moms experiencing symptoms of the baby blues recover quickly and remain well.

» **Having the baby blues means that I'm not bonding well with my baby.**

The baby blues usually don't lead to trouble with bonding. Since symptoms tend to be short-lived, and most of the time moms feel okay emotionally, bonding usually happens without any particular difficulty. It may be hard to be patient with, or to enjoy, a newborn in moments of sadness or anxiety, but the rest of the time, things usually go smoothly. Remember that bonding happens differently for all parents. Sometimes it feels like love at first sight when the baby is born, and sometimes it takes a while for those feelings to take root.

» **My mom and sister both had pretty intense baby blues, so I'll probably get it too.**

Though there is a hereditary link for post-partum mood and anxiety symptoms, not all family members will have the same challenges. If you have relatives who have had baby blues or postpartum depression and anxiety, it's a good idea to focus on strategies to maintain your mental health as soon as the baby is born.

» **The baby blues are all about hormones, so I just need to wait, and everything will be okay.**

Though hormones likely play a role in the baby blues, they are not the sole cause.

Rather than just try to ride it out, the PARENTS guidelines below can help you to focus on self-care and getting support so that it will be less of a struggle. Good self-care while experiencing the baby blues may decrease the likelihood of symptoms progressing to postpartum depression or anxiety.

PARENTS and the Baby Blues

Let's apply the PARENTS method to the baby blues.

 Practice Patience

A lot has changed since bringing home the baby. It's understandable to feel out of sorts and over-whelmed. Take a deep breath and give yourself the grace to get through these hard first weeks. Rest assured that things will get easier as the baby gets older.

 Activities for Yourself

It's important to let your body have time to heal. Though you may feel the urge to get up and get busy, slow down and take your time at first. In these early weeks with a newborn, lots of physical activity may not be feasible or safe. If you can, carve out some time for quiet enjoyable activities, like reading, journaling, chatting with a friend, listening to a podcast, or enjoying take-out from all those new restaurants you've meant to try.

R Rest and Sleep

Rest and sleep are important, but they are hard to come by when you have a newborn. Slow down and rest or nap during the day to let your body recover. Overnight, enlist your co-parent to share duties or ask a friend or family member to come over to help so that you can get some longer stretches of sleep in between feedings. If you have the means, a night nanny or post-partum doula can be helpful. Many people don't have access to such support, so if those options won't work for you, focus on doing what you can to get through each night and make sure to set aside adequate rest time during the day. For example, when your baby is sleeping/napping, take that time to rest (even if you don't actually sleep). Remember that eventually, all babies will start to sleep for longer, continuous hours at night. This early newborn stage won't last forever.

 ## Exercise and Movement

Many women won't be medically cleared to exercise by their doctor or midwife until at least 6 weeks postpartum. In the weeks before that, exercise might look more like a casual walk around the block or the mall. If the weather in your area allows for it, a great option is a 15 to 30 minute walk with your baby in a stroller right before the baby's nap time. Doing some type of movement every day is a good goal, but keep in mind that your body needs to heal, so be gentle with yourself and take it slow.

 ## Nutrition

Having a newborn can feel like all work and no play, with little time for the basics, like cooking and eating. It's easy for parents to miss meals because they are attending to the baby. Consider making food ahead of time and freezing it or having someone set up a meal train so friends and family can pitch in to bring meals some days. Help with food shopping and meal preparation are great ways to enlist the help of your support system.

T Time with Others

With a super cute new baby around, you'll likely have many visitors and lots of people asking to come by to meet the baby. Some social time is important so that you don't feel isolated. When you're home with a baby all day, adult conversation can be a real blessing. That said, too many guests can feel overwhelming, and the last thing you should be expected to do is entertain.

A great option for quick "meet the baby" moments is using technology to connect with local or faraway friends and family. Platforms like Zoom, Facetime, and Skype make it easy for someone to meet the baby for a few minutes. This approach can be less daunting to the parents and can decrease the number of visitors coming to your home.

Another good rule to enforce is to keep visits short. As one author's brother is famous for saying, "the best visitors are the ones who bring food and stay for 15 minutes." If someone offers to bring something when they visit, always take them up on it. Visitors can bring food, diapers, extra toilet paper, or laundry soap – whatever would be helpful. A good skill to work on is getting comfortable with saying "no" to visitors if you're exhausted or just not in the mood. It's taxing to have a constant stream of company. Among other reasons, it can get in the way of using some of the other PARENTS strategies, which we know can help things go well.

Finally, it's worthwhile for new parents to practice the graceful guest dismissal so that when those 15 minutes of visiting are up, you can confidently and guiltlessly stand up, open the door, and say, "Well, it was great to see you and so glad you stopped by; we've got to do this again. Thanks so much for the food and see you soon!"

S Support Network

It takes a village: that saying is true when it comes to newborns. Give yourself permission to *not* do everything on your own. Ask for and accept help in all forms. Get comfortable with sharing your to-do lists with your support people. If you've got a support network, they'll be happy to pitch in, and–a bonus–asking for small favors turns out to be a great way to build relationships because it's a bonding experience to work together or to work on someone's behalf. Plus, people love to be considered the helpful auntie/uncle/grandparent when they make your life easier. Lots of times, support people want to "help" by holding the baby, which is great for a little while, but don't be shy about asking them to also help with unloading the dishwasher, running an errand, folding laundry, or shoveling snow/mowing the lawn. Babies are a lot of work, and the more hands on deck, the better.

Revisiting Monica

After two weeks, Monica was feeling better. Though caring for a newborn was demanding, and she felt tired most days, she had settled into a routine. She no longer experienced the unexpected flares of emotion and was much less irritable. She asked for help from her mother and sister; one of them would come over during the day to help around the house and to keep Monica company. As her baby grew, Monica became more comfortable with breastfeeding, so this was no longer a stressor. She started *going for walks with the baby and made sure to have some time to herself since alone time was always something refreshing for her. In the evenings, after the baby was bathed, she would cozy up in her bed and listen to her favorite podcast. Monica's experience in those first two weeks is typical and common. With time, support, and practice, she found her way as a new mom.*

CHAPTER 4

THE EDINBURGH POSTNATAL DEPRESSION SCALE

The Edinburgh Postnatal Depression Scale (EPDS) is a commonly used and well-validated questionnaire that screens for perinatal depression (Cox & Sagovsky, 1987). It can be used during pregnancy or postpartum and consists of 10 questions about emotional experiences, including feelings of depression and anxiety. It has also been validated for screening dads and other non-birth parents.

In recent years, several organizations have put forth clear recommendations that all women should be screened for depression and anxiety throughout pregnancy and postpartum. This is often done with the EPDS, but there are other screening tools as well. The choice of which screening questionnaire is used may vary at different medical facilities. If your OB/GYN, midwife, family medicine doctor, or pediatrician doesn't give you an EPDS or other screening tool, ask to be screened. Otherwise, complete the EPDS in this chapter and bring it to your doctor's appointment to start a conversation and plan to get help.

The EPDS is also available online, including versions that have automatic scoring. Additionally, the EPDS has been translated into many languages.

Here it is in English.

As you are pregnant or have recently had a baby, we would like to know how you are feeling. Please check the answer that comes closest to how you have felt in the past 7 days, not just how you feel today.

In the past 7 days:

1. **I have been able to laugh and see the funny side of things.**

    ☐ As much as I always could

    ☐ Not quite so much now

    ☐ Definitely not so much now

    ☐ Not at all

2. **I have looked forward with enjoyment to things.**

☐ As much as I ever did

☐ Rather less than I used to

☐ Definitely less than I used to

☐ Hardly at all

*3. **I have blamed myself unnecessarily when things went wrong.**

☐ Yes, most of the time

☐ Yes, some of the time

☐ Not very often

☐ No, never

4. **I have been anxious or worried for no good reason.**

☐ No, not at all

☐ Hardly ever

☐ Yes, sometimes

☐ Yes, very often

*5. I have felt scared or panicky for no very good reason.

☐ Yes, quite a lot

☐ Yes, sometimes

☐ No, not much

☐ No, not at all

*6. Things have been getting on top of me.

☐ Yes, most of the time, I haven't been able to cope at all

☐ Yes, sometimes I haven't been coping as well as usual

☐ No, most of the time, I have coped quite well

☐ No, I have been coping as well as ever

*7. I have been so unhappy that I have had difficulty sleeping.

☐ Yes, most of the time

☐ Yes, sometimes

☐ Not very often

☐ No, not at all

*8. I have felt sad and miserable.

- ☐ Yes, most of the time
- ☐ Yes, quite often
- ☐ Not very often
- ☐ No, not at all

*9. I have been so unhappy that I have been crying.

- ☐ Yes, most of the time
- ☐ Yes, quite often
- ☐ Only occasionally
- ☐ No, never

*10. The thought of harming myself has occurred to me.

- ☐ Yes, quite often
- ☐ Sometimes
- ☐ Hardly ever
- ☐ Never

Scoring the EPDS

Questions 1, 2, and 4 (those without an *) are scored 0, 1, 2, 3 in order, with the top option scored as 0 and the bottom option scored as 3.

Questions 3 and 5-10 (those with an *) are scored in reverse order, with the top option scored as 3 and the bottom option as 0.

Maximum score: 30

A total score of 10-13 indicates *possible* depression.

A total score of 14 or higher indicates *probable* depression.

What to Do If You Score 10 or Higher?

The EPDS is a screening tool: getting a score of 10 or more does not necessarily mean you have a diagnosis of depression or anxiety. Still, it does mean you should contact your health care professional to talk more about what you're experiencing. This could be your OB/GYN or midwife, your primary care doctor, your child's pediatrician, or your mental health clinician if you already have one. Reaching out to a professional is particularly important if you marked anything other than 0 on item #10, which asks about thoughts of harming yourself.

Though the EPDS is not formally broken down into subtests, it can be helpful to look at some questions individually. After having a baby, many women report feeling more anxious than depressed. For these women, it's possible to have a total EPDS score of less than 10 but still feel like they're not their usual self. If you took the EPDS above, there are some specific questions that will give a better sense of possible anxiety symptoms.

What did you score on the following questions?

> » Question 4: _____
>
> » Question 5: _____
>
> » Question 6: _____
>
> » TOTAL: _____

If you scored 2 or 3 on one of these questions, or have a total score of 5 or higher, it may indicate that you are feeling more anxious rather than depressed. In this case, it would also be a good idea to reach out and talk to your healthcare professional.

It's important that all women get screened for depression and anxiety during pregnancy and postpartum. The EPDS is one tool for screening. It can help us pick up on symptoms that might be missed, which can lead to delays in treatment and recovery. If we pay attention to these symptoms in a timely fashion, we can get going on treatment and help parents feel like themselves again.

CHAPTER 5

DEPRESSION

Patient Story - Alecia

We met Alecia when her second child was 7 months old. She had scored 15 on the Edinburgh Postnatal Depression Scale during an appointment with her midwife (see Chapter 4 for more on the EPDS). Her midwife talked to her about the screening score and helped her make an appointment with a therapist and psychiatrist. Now a second-time mom, Alecia hadn't been coping well. She thought that she would "just get used to having two little ones" and that her mood would improve on its own. But it hadn't. She recalled her symptoms starting when her baby was about 1 month old. Alecia reported feeling sad, anxious, overwhelmed all the time, irritable and short-tempered, and having diffi-

culty concentrating and making decisions. She would describe her anxiety as a sense of feeling "frozen" or immobilized by her symptoms. She also had significant difficulty sleeping and never felt well-rested even though the baby was finally sleeping through the night. Alecia felt lots of guilt because her sad and anxious mood prevented her from spending time with her children in the ways she wanted. She often didn't find parenting fun and only occasionally enjoyed her role as a mother.

Postpartum Depression: The Basics

Many times, people come to a first appointment with us and say something like, "I'm not myself." What they are saying is that something has changed, and they no longer are feeling and coping like they normally would. Depression can be hard to define when it's the first time you've experienced it. With postpartum depression, parents feel torn between these sad, anxious, angry, or apathetic feelings and the boundless joy that society says they *should* feel about having a baby. As a result, many people don't ask for help, or they ignore their feelings, hoping that things will get better on their own, which doesn't always happen. Feeling depressed after having a baby often leaves people feeling confused and like a failure: "I'm a terrible parent because a good parent wouldn't feel this way about their baby."

It is estimated that at least 15% of women (1 in 7) will experience postpartum depression, making it one of the most common birth complications in the U.S. (Postpartum Support International, 2021). Rates of PPD may be twice that for women of color (Howell, Mora, Horowitz & Leventhal, 2005) and women of color have been shown to be less likely, for a variety of reasons, to seek treatment (Kozhimannil, Trinacty, Busch, Huskamp, & Adams, 2011). Additionally, we know that many women may not recognize or report symptoms so these numbers may even be an underestimate.

For some parents, the symptoms of depression start while they are still pregnant. If that's the case, they should definitely talk to their healthcare clinicians. We want all parents to feel well as soon as possible, and depression during pregnancy may raise the risk of mood struggles during the postpartum period. Fortunately, we know that treating mental health concerns during pregnancy can help to protect against developing postpartum depression and anxiety.

Typical Symptoms of Postpartum Depression

It is common for everyone to feel some of the symptoms listed below for short periods. However, a clinical diagnosis of depression means that you experience many of these symptoms, most of the time, for at least 2 weeks (American Psychiatric Association, 2013). The symptoms typical of postpartum depression are:

» **Sad mood**

Sadness can come in several forms: feeling down, blue, unhappy, or depressed.

» **Crying spells**

Crying spells may be sporadic or more constant. They may be triggered by something specific or seem to come out of the blue. Unlike the crying that people tend to have with the baby blues (see Chapter 3), these tearful spells tend to linger and persist.

» **Intense irritability, anger, or mood swings**

The irritability and anger that can come with postpartum depression often surprises new moms since we don't typically associate these feelings with the sadness people expect with depression. This type of irritability is often quick and unexpected, leading the parent to feel like her emotions are out of control. Also, these angry reactions often feel more intense than the situation might be expected to provoke.

» **Insomnia**

We know that sleep is disrupted with a new baby, but this sleep problem is more than that. We routinely ask if parents can sleep when the baby is sleeping or when someone else is taking care of the baby. Parents struggling with postpartum depression will often say that they can't sleep even when they have the opportunity, despite being physically and mentally exhausted.

» **Loss of appetite or overeating**

When depressed, some people find that they lose their appetite, and others overeat. If your eating habits have changed and/or seem related to your emotional state, that's often a sign of depression.

» **Overwhelming fatigue**

This is fatigue and exhaustion beyond what we would expect from disrupted sleep due to having a baby. All new parents feel tired, but those struggling with postpartum depression may experience fatigue that is debilitating and gets in the way of accomplishing basic daily tasks. They often feel this extreme level of tiredness even after getting a full night's sleep.

» **Loss of interest**

Depression often leads to people losing interest in or not enjoying things that they would normally. This might be a loss of interest in the baby or older children, but often, it is losing interest in your hobbies, relationships, work, or favorite other activities.

» **Intrusive thoughts**

Intrusive thoughts are unwanted thoughts that seem to pop into your mind without warning. They are typically upsetting or negative in nature like envisioning an accident or injury happening to the baby or other family member. Research suggests that approximately 40% of women with postpartum depression will experience these types of thoughts at a clinically significant level (Abramowitz et al., 2010). Because the thoughts are frequent and sometimes repetitive, many parents worry that these bad things will happen in real life.

» **Difficulty making decisions**

With postpartum depression, this indecisive-ness is often described as feeling "frozen" when faced with a decision – even a simple decision, like which color pajamas to put on the baby, can be immobilizing. Depression fre-quently leaves a person's mind feeling foggy, slow, and unable to focus and concentrate.

» **Withdrawal from family and friends**

Pulling away from friends and family is a common experience with depression. With postpartum depression, new parents often feel like they have to "put on a mask" of hap-piness. When people feel down, they often retreat because social situations can feel overwhelming and exhausting. Unfortunately, this tendency to isolate usually makes the person's depression worse, causing them to withdraw even more. For new parents, this might look like not leaving the house for several days or longer, ignoring calls and texts from friends and family, or staying in the bedroom when the rest of the family is watching a movie together.

» **Guilt and negative thoughts about parenting ability**

A nearly universal experience for people struggling with postpartum depression is having negative thoughts and guilt about their parenting skills. People describe feeling like a failure and worry that they are making mistakes that will negatively affect their child forever. This can feel particularly intense for first-time parents since everything about caring for a baby is unfamiliar.

» **Ambivalent or negative thoughts toward the baby**

Postpartum depression sometimes comes with a lack of interest in the new baby or feeling poorly bonded with the baby, but not always. Bonding with a newborn isn't instantaneous for all parents. However, if these feelings of disconnection persist, they could be related to postpartum depression.

» **Thoughts of harming yourself or the baby**

Sometimes, if depression becomes bad enough, people may have thoughts about harming themselves, about suicide, or about harming their baby. New parents sometimes have thoughts of wanting to run away and escape, leaving the family and driving to another state, for example. If someone is having thoughts of hurting themselves or their baby, they should seek help right away. They can call 911, a national suicide prevention hotline, or their doctor. If there are concerns about suicide or violence, the first priority is to get help. Chapter 15 of this book includes some resources that are available for people in crisis.

When most people think of postpartum depression, they typically envision someone who is sad, crying, or unable to get out of bed or take care of their baby. For some people, that's what it looks like. However, for many others, they feel more on edge with disorganized/anxious energy (Wenzel, et al., 2005). These parents will care for their baby well but, in focusing so much on the child, little energy is left for other things, like taking care of themselves, work, or relationships. This difference is important because many people who experience the latter type of postpartum depression often don't ask for help or even recognize what they are experiencing. They often say, "I didn't think I had postpartum depression because I wanted to be around my baby." If the symptoms described above are getting in the way of your functioning in any important area—not just childcare—you may be experiencing depression.

The symptoms of postpartum depression can start anytime. Some people notice them right away, within a few days or weeks of giving birth. Some people feel fine until several months after the baby is born. Others will say that the symptoms started many months later (for example, after stopping breastfeeding). Depression symptoms starting anytime within 12 months of the birth of a child can be considered to be postpartum depression (Postpartum Support International, 2021).

When to Reach Out to Your Healthcare Professional

» If you are experiencing many of the depression symptoms listed above.

» If these symptoms are present much of the day and you notice that they are getting in the way of you doing the things you want and need to do.

» If these symptoms are affecting your ability to enjoy your life.

» If you are having thoughts of wanting to die or of hurting yourself or someone else. In this situation, you should contact your doctor right away.

Causes and Contributing Factors

There are several factors that predispose someone to experience postpartum depression. These can include a personal history of depression or anxiety (especially if this occurred with a previous pregnancy), alcohol or drug use, a personal history of significant premenstrual syndrome or premenstrual dysphoric disorder, a history of traumatic experiences, relationship stress or instability, lack of social support, financial strain, employment stress, unplanned pregnancy, teen pregnancy, or pregnancy complicated by things like severe nausea, previous miscarriages, fertility challenges, or a worrisome fetal diagnosis.

Other factors that may affect mental well-being include hormonal changes when restarting birth control or stopping breastfeeding, thyroid problems or changes in immune functioning, a difficult or traumatic birth, premature birth, a baby in the NICU, a baby with health complications, having multiples (twins, triplets, etc.), breastfeeding difficulties, having a baby with a difficult temperament or colic, or having a high-needs older child. Additionally, emotional factors such as anxiety about caring for the newborn, sleep deprivation, a sense of loss of control, or a struggle with one's sense of identity can also contribute to depression and anxiety.

Medication changes may be a contributor. It is well established that stopping an antidepressant medication during pregnancy or just prior to delivery increases the risk of perinatal psychological symptoms. Up to 2/3 of women who stop their medication will have symptoms return, many within just a few weeks (Cohen et al., 2006).

One particular stressor that seems to present itself fairly often is breastfeeding challenges. It could be milk supply issues, trouble with the baby's latch, pain, mastitis, the time demands for a baby that wants to eat seemingly constantly, or the time it takes to both nurse and pump. Difficulties like these can significantly affect a mother's experience with breastfeeding. These challenges typically bring on stress that can lead to depression and self-doubt, anger about her body, or resentment toward the baby. It can become a vicious cycle: feedings don't go well, which leads the mom to feel stressed and upset, which in turn negatively affects future feedings.

It's important to give the mother and baby time to adjust to breastfeeding but also make sure that she has breastfeeding support. Many women assume that since breastfeeding is "natural," it should be a piece of cake right away but that's often not the case. A woman who wants to breastfeed should be patient with herself and her baby; they both have to learn how to nurse effectively. It's important that she gets support and does not struggle for days or weeks with pain or low supply. If she is simply told to "keep doing what you are doing," she is not getting good advice and needs to talk to someone else. Getting support from a lactation consultant is a good option. Her pediatrician may or may not have training in lactation care, but may refer to a lactation specialist. If, after seeking skilled care and not being able to resolve the problem, breastfeeding is contributing to a woman's symptoms of depression or anxiety, it may be time to consider adjusting the feeding plan. We believe strongly in breastfeeding when it works so we advocate for skilled lactation support. But the overriding goal is to have a physically and mentally healthy mom, which is essential to having a healthy baby.

Patient Story - Denise

We met Denise after her third daughter was born; her baby was 10 weeks old, and her other children were 6 and 3 years old. She was referred to us by her long-time OB/GYN. Her husband is in the military and was deployed during the birth of their first daughter, returning when she was 4 months old. He was deployed again within 6 weeks post-birth of their second and third children. Denise had a history of depression – she'd had a previous episode when she was in college and she recalled feeling sad after her first child was born. She'd managed pretty well but acting as a solo parent with three young children contributed to her depression recurring. Additionally, she was one of the primary caregivers for her middle-aged mother, who had serious chronic health concerns.

Starting in her third trimester, Denise began feeling sad and irritable. She was quick to cry, felt unmotivated and exhausted, had difficulty concentrating, and was frequently forgetful. She experienced intense guilty feelings about not being a good enough parent. She spoke about these experiences with her OB/GYN, who helped with a referral to the mental health department.

Misunderstandings About Postpartum Depression

In this section, we want to dispel some of the misunderstandings people have about postpartum depression, many of which lead parents to avoid seeking help when they should.

» **Postpartum depression is just like typical "clinical depression" and usually starts right after the baby is born.**

There are many similarities between postpartum depression and other types of depression, but there are differences too. For example, in non-postpartum depression, one of the first clues that something is wrong may be disruption in sleep patterns. For postpartum parents, sleep patterns are usually already quite disrupted by the baby. As noted above, when parents can't sleep even when they have the opportunity, then that's a cause for concern for postpartum depression. Another difference is that postpartum women may feel more irritable than sad. While depression and anxiety sometimes go together, that combination is even more common in postpartum depression.

An episode of depression is often considered "postpartum depression" when it comes on anytime in the first 12 months after the baby is born. The DSM-5 (Diagnostic and Statistical Manual of Mental Disorders, 5th Ed.), which is the standard for defining psychiatric diagnoses, considers "postpartum onset" to be up to 4 weeks after the baby is born. Still, in clinical practice, it's relatively common for symptoms to first occur or first be recognized well after that 4-week mark.

» **If a parent is struggling with postpartum depression, others will be able to see it and help her.**

Many parents are able to hold it together well enough that others may not realize they have depression. Sometimes, even the parent themself doesn't recognize it until long after the baby is born or until symptoms become more severe. That's a major reason why screening for postpartum depression using tools like the EPDS is recommended. Postpartum depression is highly treatable, and the sooner treatment starts, the sooner parents can start to feel like themselves again.

» **If a person has postpartum depression, it means that she doesn't love her baby and won't bond well.**

One of the biggest struggles for parents with postpartum depression is that they love their babies as much as any parent, but the depression makes it hard to enjoy the baby or to feel like they have the energy to be present for their child. Newborns are hard; they're cute, and we love them, but they need a lot from us, and that can be exhausting when you're already not feeling great. When depression sets in, parents can feel unmotivated and find it hard to have the same positive experience they usually would as they manage parenting duties. Even though bonding can feel like more of a challenge when someone is depressed, it won't permanently alter the relationship with their baby; bonding will still happen. However, it is much easier to get back on track if the depression gets treated. Once parents get treatment, they often say they have more energy again and look forward to being around the baby.

» **Postpartum depression will resolve on its own once the parent feels more comfortable taking care of a baby.**

By definition, postpartum depression is a medical condition that interferes with a person's usual functioning, and it usually requires some type of treatment to improve. It's true that some parents may eventually feel better without treatment, but it can take a long time for that to happen, and the costs of just waiting for a resolution in symptoms may be high. All new parents have some natural anxieties about caring for a newborn, but PPD is not just first-time-parent jitters – parents with PPD deserve good medical and psychological care to get back to themselves.

» **I've seen stories in the news. It seems like postpartum depression causes parents to hurt their babies.**

Stories of parents harming their babies make the news because they're extremely rare events. If this were commonplace, it wouldn't be newsworthy. The parents in these news stories usually don't have typical postpartum depression; there are often other very significant contributing issues. For example, drug or alcohol use could be present, or postpartum psychosis (an illness that involves losing touch with reality) may be the diagnosis. Thankfully, postpartum psychosis is an extremely rare condition that affects only 1 or 2 of every 1000 new moms (Postpartum Support International, 2021). If we consider that at least 15% of new moms in the United States will develop postpartum depression(that is, hundreds of thousands of moms every year), it puts into perspective that we don't see hundreds of thousands of children being harmed by their mothers every year. So the math just doesn't add up - postpartum depression alone does not mean that babies are at risk for being harmed.

PARENTS and Postpartum Depression

Let's apply the PARENTS method to postpartum depression for some approaches to managing these symptoms.

 Practice Patience

Give yourself time to recover from childbirth and to get adjusted to this major change in your life. Be patient with yourself as you learn the ropes of parenting a newborn, or a newborn plus an older child/children. If you are having postpartum depression symptoms, get treatment – you'll feel better, and parenting will get back on track. Sometimes people worry that having depression is a personal failure – it's not. It's an illness like many others – it can be compared in many ways to things like diabetes or high blood pressure, and we'd never hesitate to get treatment for those conditions because we recognize how important our health is to our overall wellbeing and our ability to function at our best.

Something that can help you be more patient with yourself is to think back 2 to 3 weeks. What was hard/new/overwhelming then? We would bet that some of those baby-related tasks feel more natural or automatic now. For example, if you've never changed a diaper before you bring home your own baby, by week 2 you can likely do it with your eyes closed. Being patient with ourselves is so much about being patient with the learning process. No parent has things mastered after only a few weeks or months.

Activities for Yourself

Getting involved with activities you enjoy can be challenging, even unappealing, when you have depression. If you can enlist the help of a support person to join you, they can not only be good company but can help to hold you accountable for keeping up with life outside of childcare. When people have depression, they don't feel like themselves, and returning to the activities you love can start you on a path to finding yourself again. This doesn't have to be an enormous undertaking – sometimes, just sitting down with a book or seeing a movie can be enough to add some variety to your day and help life feel more enjoyable. If there are groups, teams, or organizations that you've been a part of before kids, consider returning to them. If there's a new hobby you've always wanted to try, this is a great time to do it. Also, consider how you might modify a well-established hobby to accommodate life with children.

 Rest and Sleep

This may require some negotiation with your co-parent or other support people. It's important to get a decent amount of sleep to start feeling better. As we've described in other sections of this book, it doesn't have to be 8 hours at a stretch, but if you can put together a couple of blocks of 2 to 4 hours, that may be enough to keep you going through the day until your baby learns to sleep for longer stretches. You may want to consider taking shifts in getting up with the baby or alternating nights. Here's how alternating can work: if mom is breastfeeding, and it's her night to get up with the baby, she does it all—feeding, maybe pumping, diapering, rocking—for one whole night. The next night, it's her co-parent/support person's turn – they do the diapering and rocking, and when the baby is hungry, they bring the baby to mom, who stays in bed and nurses the baby lying down, staying as close to sleep as she can, and then gets to go right back to sleep after feeding. If bottle-feeding, it can be even easier for the co-parent to take over all the baby duties on those alternate nights.

 Exercise and Movement

You may not be cleared for regular exercise by your OB/GYN or midwife for several weeks after the baby is born. In the meantime, try to be active in your everyday life. A couple extra laps up and down stairs, a gentle walk around the block, any kind of movement will help. Also consider trying low-intensity yoga, which can be great for the mind and the still-healing postpartum body. Once cleared to do more exercise, it can be tremendously helpful to build it into your routine. This doesn't mean you need to rush out to buy expensive equipment or join a gym or exercise 7 days a week. Brisk walks around the block a couple times per week, taking the stairs instead of the elevator at your apartment, anything that gets your heart rate up; it all counts as exercise. Traditional things we think of as exercise (running, playing sports, biking, taking an exercise class) are also great options. Lots of research shows that exercise can be an effective antidepressant; some studies even seem to show it can help as much as medications (Netz, 2017).

 Nutrition

There's no secret dietary regimen that helps mental health, but it does appear that eating well in general can be of benefit. There is plenty of research looking at what constitutes "eating well" and plenty of debate over different specialized diets. Still, it's probably sufficient to simply aim for eating lots of whole foods, few processed foods, low added sugars, lots of fruits and vegetables, lean proteins, and healthy fats.

One way to work towards healthy eating is to plan ahead. If you have some time early in the week, make a casserole or veggie lasagna that you can reheat during the week. This can save some time and keep you on track with eating well. Or prepare a stack of sandwiches for the upcoming week so you can eat one-handed while you're bouncing the baby. When people ask if they can bring food for your family, say yes and ask for simple, easy-to-prepare, and easy-to-eat snacks or meals.

T Time with Others

When was the last time you spent some quality time with your partner or a friend? If it's been a while, be intentional about planning something for the near future. For moms who need to breastfeed frequently, time with other adults may be brief in the early stages of parenting, or the baby may need to come along to activities, but this is still a worthwhile effort. Time together as a couple can help the midnight feedings and sleep deprivation feel more like a team effort. Are there friends you haven't seen in weeks?

Pick a date and get together for coffee, with kids or without – just make sure you're able to get some adult conversation time. Are there family members you enjoy spending time with? See if they can get together so you can catch up. Sometimes it can be helpful to get some parenting perspective from your own parents or other trusted mentors. Don't hesitate to connect virtually. If in-person meetups are not possible or important support people live far away, set up a regular video call.

 Support Network

Your family and friends may be your primary support network, but because parenting can be hard, especially if you are struggling with depression, you may need more than just them. Consider joining an online parent community – there are lots out there, and connecting through social media, for example, can be a lot more convenient than trying to plan an outing or get-together. There are some specialized online parenting networks, so cast a wide net to find the right group(s) for you.

For people who have depression, an in-person or virtual support group can also be helpful. One of the hardest parts about being depressed is that people often assume they must be the only one feeling bad. Especially when it comes to parenting, there may be some shame or embarrassment about having depression. After all, everyone says having a baby is supposed to be pure joy, right? When you want honesty and frank discussion about what it feels like to have postpartum depression, then a group of other moms who understand it, because they're going through it too, can feel like especially good company.

Revisiting Alecia

Alecia decided to pursue both individual psychotherapy and antidepressants. In therapy, she explored her feelings of guilt and her harsh, critical inner voice. After several weeks, she started to feel better. Though she still had stressors in her life, after 3 months, she was feeling back to her "usual self" and enjoying time with her two sons and partner. Alecia had a strong network of social supports – her partner and mother were key figures, and she was also part of a close-knit online moms group. Alecia stayed in regular therapy and continued taking an antidepressant medication because she found it helpful. She knew that they would like to have a third child, and she wanted that to go as smoothly as possible. When she got pregnant again, her mood was stable. In therapy, she worked on maintaining her mood and continuing to manage her anxiety. She and her therapist developed a plan for coping after the baby was born. Alecia had a healthy baby girl and never struggled with depression and anxiety during this pregnancy or postpartum.

Alecia's story is typical of postpartum depression. Though parents may know something is "off," they sometimes wait to see if things improve on their own, as Alecia did. Her sadness also came with a great deal of anxiety and feelings of being overwhelmed, which is a common experience. Her story of recovery is noteworthy; she is an example of how, with treatment, women can recover from postpartum depression, and with support and planning, future pregnancies can be a better experience.

Revisiting Denise

Denise started in individual therapy. She worked on establishing social supports and a routine to help her manage her day-to-day tasks, given that her husband would be deployed for several more months. She also focused on the excessive guilt she was feeling and worked with her therapist to develop skills to confront these negative, self-critical thoughts and to have a more balanced view of herself and her skills as a mother and to increase her confidence in her ability to manage the children on her own. This was important because she knew that her husband would be away from the family again in the future. After several months, Denise's mood improved, and she became more confident in her ability to cope with stressful situations.

CHAPTER 6

POSTPARTUM DEPRESSION IN THEIR OWN WORDS

In previous chapters, you've read examples of the types of parents we typically work with, and we hope their stories and experiences have been useful in understanding postpartum mood and anxiety symptoms. In this chapter, you'll hear directly from some of our patients. They share what it was like for them to struggle with depression and/or anxiety, how they knew they should ask for help, and what getting treatment was like. These are their experiences and opinions. We hope that you find them inspiring and feel reassured through their stories that things can get better.

Alecia

Were there times you didn't feel like your usual self? What were those times like? How did you know something was different?

There were definitely times I didn't feel like my usual self, although I don't know that I thought of it that way at the time. Between being sick during my pregnancy and then having to recover from giving birth and adjusting to being a mother of two, I didn't really know what my "usual self" felt like; I think that made it harder for me to recognize when I started going into the depression.

When did you know that you needed to ask for help? Who did you go to first? What did that person do or say that was helpful?

I knew I needed to ask for help when I just wasn't feeling any motivation to do anything other than the bare minimum. Day-to-day housework and self-care were getting ignored but so was anything that I had previously enjoyed doing. I was taking proper care of my children, and their general safety and wellbeing were being attended to, but I had a lot less patience for them, and I felt like I was missing out on being with them because of how poorly I felt. I had a lot of anxiety, which made it hard for me to do fun things with my children because I was worried something was going to go wrong or someone was going to get hurt. I think I first told my partner that I was beginning to think it was postpartum depression, and then I talked to my midwife. My midwife recommended a therapist and she helped me begin to adjust my medication while I waited to see a psychiatrist.

What did you find was most helpful for starting to feel better?

I think the thing that first helped me feel better was just doing something about it. Even before my first appointment with the therapist and before the new medication started working, I felt a lot of relief just by making the appointment and taking some action to get help.

Did you see a therapist? What was psychotherapy like? How was it helpful?

I did see a therapist, and I think that was a really important part of my treatment plan. As a mom of a toddler and an infant, I think just having someone to talk to was helpful. Seeing someone who saw a lot of moms was great because I was able to hear that I wasn't alone, and I didn't feel guilty talking about the hard parts of parenting. Together, we developed strategies to help me manage my depression and anxiety. There were also other stressful things going on in my life at the time, along with parenting a toddler and infant, and the consistent appointments were important to keep me going and prevent me from going back into the depression spiral.

Did you take medication(s)? Did you have hesitations about taking medication? If so, what were they? What was it like to take medication(s)? How did the medication(s) help you feel better?

I had already been on an SSRI (selective serotonin reuptake inhibitor - a type of antidepressant medication) for a few years before my postpartum depression symptoms, but I knew that I needed a change in dose or medication. I did have some hesitation because I was breastfeeding and worried about medications being safe to use. Originally, my midwife adjusted one of my medications, and that was helpful because I had gotten to know her throughout my pregnancy. I trusted that she would not prescribe anything that would be harmful. She was also very easy to get an appointment with, so I was able to start the medication changes right away while I was waiting for my first therapist appointment. I then saw a psychiatrist who specializes in treating pregnant and postpartum patients, which was so helpful because she was so knowledgeable about safety and risks. If I were ever concerned about medication, she would take the time to go over any studies or data that would help me put my mind at ease or help me make any decisions. It was also important because when we decided to have another child, I was able to talk to her about medications during pregnancy, and we were able to come up with a plan in case I developed postpartum depression/anxiety again.

What advice would you give to parents who are experiencing mental health difficulties after their baby is born?

My biggest piece of advice is that asking for help can be really hard, but it's so important, and there are people that want to help you. When you are in the middle of feeling depressed and even taking a shower can seem like a heavy task, taking a big step like that can be so daunting. But after you ask for help, it gets easier because you are not doing it alone. It's also important to remember that there are a lot of places where you can start getting help, including online resources where you don't have to talk to anyone face to face. Online support groups or places where you can chat with other parents going through the same thing can be so helpful for things like finding resources or just knowing you're not alone.

Are there other things you would like to share about your experience with postpartum depression?

I think another important thing for people experiencing postpartum depression to remember is that it's okay if the first (or second or third) therapist you see isn't the right fit. It's okay to keep looking. Find someone who you will be able to be the most honest with and who you *want* to see. You can't get the help you need if you aren't motivated to go to your appointments or if you don't feel like you can be truthful with your therapist.

Denise

Were there times when you didn't feel like your usual self? What were those times like? How did you know something was different?

After my third daughter was born, I had a difficult time engaging with any of my children. I was emotionally numb most of the time and felt like I was just existing from one task to the next. I had experienced something similar to this before, after the birth of my first daughter, and knew that was not what I wanted to feel like again. I didn't feel any happiness, and I realized that the only strong emotions I felt anymore were overwhelming frustration and guilt, but the overarching emotion was numbness. Because I knew logically that was not how I was supposed to be feeling, I ended up acting happy and excited around other people because that was expected, and that just left me exhausted, which contributed to the numbness. I felt weak and helpless, and I felt like this was something I could (and previously had) handled and dealt with on my own. I felt like I was somehow "less" because I couldn't deal with it. I looked around and saw other people dealing with much harder issues than having a baby, and working through things just fine. I just couldn't understand why I felt so stuck in my numbness.

When did you know that you needed to ask for help? Who did you go to first? What did that person do or say that was helpful?

When I met with my OB/GYN for my postpartum checkup, I opened up to her and told her about the issues I was having. She had been my doctor for years and had always given me good advice. She suggested that I meet with a therapist, and she had a specific person in mind that would be a good fit for me. It helped that my doctor came up with a concrete plan and helped me make that first appointment. So before I left the office, I knew the next steps I would take to get help. The fact that she was so responsive and supportive helped validate that I was struggling beyond what was normal, and the numbness and frustration weren't only in my head. It helped me feel less "crazy" and less like I was overreacting to a situation that most people could handle on their own.

What did you find the most helpful for starting to feel better?

Initially, having someone (both my OB/GYN and my therapist) just listen to me dump out all my feelings and validate that what I was dealing with was causing issues for me was cathartic. With my husband in the military, there is an understanding that you don't bother your military spouse with issues at home, especially when they are on training missions or deployed. "Your spouse cannot afford the distraction of home life": I was specifically told this at a Beyond the Yellow Ribbon family event. While I was given phone numbers and websites for support, it always felt like they were to be used for people who were at the end of their rope and shouldn't be wasted on me. So, being able to find resources handed to me by my doctors felt validating and like those resources were specifically for me.

Did you see a therapist? What was psychotherapy like? Was it helpful?

I began seeing my therapist shortly after meeting with my OB/GYN for my postpartum appointment. It was helpful to have someone listen to me, make me feel like I wasn't a burden to them, and that it was a good thing I was seeking help. My husband was frequently away from home with the military, and when he was home, he was spread thin balancing his post-graduate schooling, work, and military obligations. It felt like an extra burden to put my feelings on his already full plate. I had children earlier than my siblings and my friends, so I didn't have a great network of people who I could talk to or ask questions. My mom was critically ill at this point, and we had an occasionally tense relationship, so I didn't feel comfortable talking to her. One of the first things I learned in therapy was that some days, keeping everyone alive and fed is enough. I didn't need to be the mom that I had built up in my mind who gets everything done and is "Pinterest perfect," and, in fact, that comparison was actually hurting me. I also learned that I need to recognize my feelings and limitations as well as how important self-care is to being a better parent. It was like I needed someone to tell me that it was okay to take care of myself, which seems like a simple thing, but after so many years of being laser-focused on my kids, I had lost my own identity and needs into the *mom* persona. I also developed many grounding techniques that helped me deal with the anxiety that grew over the years, which is a huge help in making me functional daily.

Did you take medication(s)? Did you have hesitation about taking medication? If so, what were they? What was it like to take medication(s)? How did medication(s) help you feel better?

I recently started medications for both depression and anxiety. I had been on an antidepressant medication about 15 years ago and hated it. It helped with the depression, but I didn't feel anything else at all. I decided that I would rather deal with the bouts of depression if it meant that I could feel other things. I'm an emotional person, so it was difficult to handle feeling like a robot. My therapist started to help me realize that my depression and anxiety were becoming overwhelming, but I dug in my heels and refused to go on medication partly because of my past experience and honestly, partly due to my pride and belief that I didn't need it. Eventually, I found out my mom was terminal in her illness and basically had a rolling panic attack for two days before I sought out medication from urgent care. The next week, I visited my primary care physician, and we slowly added an antidepressant (different than the one I took years earlier) to help me cope. In the last 15 years, options have changed for depression and anxiety medications, and we were able to tweak and develop a plan for my specific needs. The medication I received in urgent care helped immediately to stop the panic attack, and I still occasionally use it when I feel an attack coming on and can't stop it with the grounding I do. My everyday antidepressant helps lower the anxiety and depression to a manageable level. I have tried a couple of medications that definitely did not work for me, but open communication with my doctor helps sort those issues out. I still do feel anxiety and depression, but now it is more like a subtle part of my life rather than the only personality I have.

What advice would you give to parents who are experiencing mental health difficulties after their baby is born?

Talk to your doctors, nurses, midwives, and partners about how you are feeling. If you don't feel comfortable talking to your medical team, or they aren't responsive or don't take you seriously, find new medical help. You are not crazy, and you are the best judge of things not being right. Depression doesn't have to be a dire situation before you get help. Don't ignore your feelings or experience. Medication can be a game-changer, and there are so many different options; don't be stubborn about adding them into your treatment plan.

Are there other things you would like to share about your experience with postpartum depression?

It's hard to have postpartum depression, and there was a lot of guilt for me that I couldn't just be happy with my healthy family. I honestly should have sought help with my first child and second, but expectations and pride kept me from seeking help. I assumed it felt terrible for everyone, and I was just being weak for not coping like I thought I should. I felt guilty for "wallowing" in my feelings and not just putting my head down and working through them. But the absolute relief I felt with someone objectively telling me it was okay, and I needed help, was unbelievable and helped change my life forever. I regret taking so long to make my emotional health a priority.

CHAPTER 7

ANXIETY

Patient Story - Krystal

Krystal was 36 years old when her second child was born. She started seeing a therapist and psychiatrist when she was 5 months pregnant. She had a history of anxiety since college that had generally been well-managed. The birth of her son went smoothly, and she bonded well with him. Krystal's main stressor was the high level of conflict in her blended family. She and her husband had two children together. He also had 3 children, young teenagers, from his previous marriage. The conflicts among the older kids and his ex-wife led Krystal to experience high anxiety. Her symptoms included constant worry, disrupted sleep, problems with concentration and being distracted, rumination, restlessness and feeling on edge, fatigue, and irritability. About once a week or so, she would also experience panic attack symptoms such as heart palpitations, trouble breathing, dizziness, and claustrophobia.

Postpartum Anxiety: The Basics

It is estimated that 10% to 50% of women will experience postpartum anxiety, meaning that it may be more common than postpartum depression (Wenzel, et al., 2005). Something that we've heard frequently from our patients is that they didn't tell anyone about the anxiety they were feeling. Instead they wonder, "isn't this just what motherhood is like, feeling worried all the time?" The answer is no, this is not what parenting should feel like. Of course, there will be times of nervousness and anxiety, especially for first-time parents who are trying to figure things out, but parents shouldn't expect to feel on edge all the time.

Anxiety sometimes starts during pregnancy. Worries about labor and delivery, caring for a newborn, and how much life will change can be triggers for prenatal anxiety. For women who have experienced a past miscarriage or stillbirth, a new pregnancy can bring a lot of anxiety and worries about the baby's health.

Pregnancy with a "rainbow baby" (a baby following a pregnancy loss) can lead to a mix of emotions–fear, joy, anxiety, hope. Many women in this situation find it hard to relax until the baby is born.

Typical Symptoms of Postpartum Anxiety

Having a bad day occasionally is normal. Feeling more anxious when you encounter a new stage of parenting or feeling on edge after a particularly rough night of sleep is to be expected. Like postpartum depression, anxiety is considered a clinical problem if functioning is impaired, meaning that the anxiety gets in the way of daily tasks, relationships, work, or other obligations, and it is present most days for an extended period of time, meaning it's more than just short episodes or "flare-ups." Symptoms typical of postpartum anxiety are:

Racing, ruminative thoughts

» Parents with anxiety say that they are unable to "turn their minds off." Anxious thoughts seem to bounce from one worry to the next, or the thought seems to repeat itself over and over.

Excessive worry

» Worry is frequently more intense than what the situation calls for. People find themselves worried about a lot of different things at once, including money, relationships, getting tasks accomplished, going back to work, the safety of loved ones, and many other topics, as opposed to being just focused on worries about the baby.

Inability to relax

» People may feel physically tense much of the time. Sometimes this manifests in physical complaints, like neck and backaches, headaches, and stomach problems. Or sometimes it's a general sense of being on edge.

Poor sleep

» Because it can be hard to turn off anxious thoughts, falling asleep can be a challenge. Parents find they are thinking about all the things they have to do tomorrow, how they "failed" that day, or cringe over an uncomfortable social interaction.

Fatigue

» Since sleep is often affected by anxiety, and it is physically and emotionally exhausting to feel worried and on edge much of the day, feeling run down is a common complaint. And this may be true even after getting a good night's sleep.

Irritability

» Anxiety often causes people to feel irritable or over-reactive. Sometimes this occurs because anxiety leads us to want to control things in our life in order to try to feel better. Other times an angry outburst could be the result of feeling overwhelmed because too many things are coming at you at once.

Excessive checking on the baby

» Every parent feels the urge to check on their baby when they are sleeping. Occasional checking is common and okay. However, if you find yourself checking on the baby multiple times at nighttime or naptime, when the baby hasn't cried to indicate that they need something, this could be a sign of anxiety.

Poor concentration

» With anxious thoughts bouncing around in your mind, it's easy to feel distracted. Anxiety often feels like you're holding too many things in your mind at the same time, like a juggler with multiple balls in the air. Losing track of things, being forgetful, or being unable to focus is common.

The first type of anxiety we described in this chapter is one that we can think of as generalized worry, present much of the day, about several topics. However, there are other ways anxiety can present itself after a baby is born or during pregnancy. These are described below.

Postpartum Panic Attacks

Instead of having continual unease, some parents will experience panic attacks – sudden, intense anxiety that often comes with physical symptoms. These may be short-lived, just a minute or two, or could last longer.

The percentage of mothers who experience postpartum panic disorder (a pattern of frequent panic attacks) is around 11% (Wenzel, et al., 2001).

Typical symptoms of panic attacks include:

Surge of intense fear or anxiety

» The anxiety and physical symptoms may feel like they come "out of the blue" with no warning or trigger.

Physical symptoms

» Physical symptoms of anxiety and panic can include pounding heartbeat/palpitations, sweating, trembling, shortness of breath, choking sensation, chest pain/tightness, upset stomach, dizziness, chills or hot flashes, and tingling in hands or feet.

Sense of dread, fear of dying, or fear of "going crazy"

» People who have had a panic attack often describe it as feeling like they were having a heart attack. This can also come with a sense of dread, but inability to pinpoint what the potential feared event might be. Panic symptoms often make the person feel out of control of their body and thoughts.

These symptoms usually come on suddenly and are sometimes triggered by a situation or stressor, or sometimes there seems to be no precipitating event. A panic attack usually lasts for a few minutes. They can come in isolation, or there can be multiple panic attacks clustered together. When panic attacks happen during the postpartum period, they are often triggered by fears about the baby's safety, feeling over-whelmed, or the prospect of going out of the house with the baby. Panic attacks can be scary and physically uncomfortable. Because of this, once someone has experienced one, they often worry about having another, which can unfortu-nately bring on the symptoms again.

Patient Story - Jaclyn

Jaclyn felt well for a long time after her first child was born but developed new symptoms when she was 25 weeks pregnant with her second child, a daughter. Two months earlier, she no-ticed a significant increase in anxiety, including constant worry that was difficult to control, prob-lems sleeping because she was unable to "turn her mind off" at night, problems with concentra-tion and memory, irritability, crying spells, and intense feelings of guilt. She described feeling impatient and easily irritated with her husband

and son. She said she recognized that she was overreacting in these situations but that she had trouble controlling her emotions. Her daughter was born on December 23rd, which made for a stressful holiday season for their usually festive family.

Additionally, the new baby was often fussy and difficult to soothe, which increased Jaclyn's anxiety and sense of being overwhelmed. Over time, she also began to experience panic symptoms that were triggered by fears about the safety of her husband and children. These would occur when her husband came home a few minutes late or didn't answer his cell phone. Moreover, she struggled with leaving her children at daycare, worrying that something bad would happen to them or that she was a bad mom because she was returning to work. Jaclyn frequently found herself engaging in "what if" ruminations that would spin into fears about worst-case scenarios. She felt anxious most of the day and was unable to relax and enjoy her maternity leave.

Postpartum Obsessive-Compulsive Disorder

Another way that anxiety can present itself is through obsessive thinking and compulsive behaviors. Around 2-3% of new mothers experience postpartum obsessive-compulsive disorder (OCD) (Postpartum Support International, 2021).

Typical symptoms of obsessive thinking are:

Recurrent, intrusive thoughts that cause anxiety

» These are thoughts, usually distressing in content, that pop into a person's mind unexpectedly and often repeat themselves over and over.

» The thoughts are difficult to control or ignore.

Typical symptoms of compulsive behaviors are:

Repetitive behaviors

» Examples of repetitive behaviors include hand washing, ordering/organizing, and repeated checking (for example, checking on the baby, checking that the door is locked or the oven is turned off). These behaviors are done in an attempt to reduce the anxiety caused by the intrusive thoughts.

Typically, this works for just a short time and then the anxiety returns, causing the person to repeat the behaviors again.

Repetitive mental acts

» Examples of mental acts include counting or repeating words silently. These are also meant to reduce the anxiety caused by intrusive thoughts. And like repetitive behaviors, they typically only help for a short time.

Strong urges to engage in the behaviors listed above

» These urges are a feeling of being driven to apply behavior rules, which are often rigid and inflexible, in order to avoid worsened symptoms or to avoid worst-case scenarios coming true. For example, having a rule like, "if I wash the baby's bottles in this specific way, then nothing bad will happen to him."

Many moms (perhaps up to 87%) with post-partum depression and/or anxiety symptoms report having intrusive thoughts (Abramowitz et al., 2010). These are upsetting and unwanted thoughts that pop into your mind unexpectedly. Sometimes they are triggered by a specific experience, and other times they feel like they come out of the blue.

When conceptualizing the word *thought*, we usually think of it as a quick idea. However, with intrusive thoughts, many women describe them more like little movies that play over and over in their minds. They often have a great deal of detail. Because they are so detailed, these upsetting thoughts can feel very real. Intrusive thoughts tend to fall into a few categories:

» Fear of the baby dying while sleeping

» Harm coming to the child with a knife or by shaking

» Accidents or mistakes (often committed by a parent) leading to injury or death

» Sexual misconduct involving the child

» Fear that the baby will be contaminated by germs or chemicals

These thoughts can be daunting to talk about, especially to a healthcare provider. Parents experiencing these thoughts often feel guilty, scared, and worried that they would be judged if they share what they've been thinking. In most cases, these thoughts are a symptom of the anxiety, and the baby is not in danger.

A Note on "OCD"

The term "OCD" is used frequently in casual conversation. Most of the time, when non-clinicians use it, they are describing experiences of a person who is rigid in behaviors and expectations about things like cleanliness or orderliness, but that's not what clinicians mean when they diagnose OCD. It's normal to double-check that your front door is locked before you go to bed, to reorganize your pantry occasionally, or to check on the baby when she is sleeping. A formal diagnosis of OCD involves doing these types of behaviors repeatedly to the extent that they significantly interfere with daily functioning. It also usually means the behaviors are driven by a seemingly irresistible urge and done in an attempt to reduce anxiety. The thoughts and behaviors are often time-consuming and get in the way of the person living their life and performing their usual daily tasks.

When to Reach Out to
Your Healthcare Professional

» If you've experienced symptoms like the ones described in this chapter, and it feels like they're getting in your way of you enjoying your life and your new baby, check in with a healthcare clinician.

» If you find that repetitive behaviors or mental acts take up an excessive amount of your time during the day or prevent you from doing the things you need to do, reach out for help. These symptoms can be reduced with effective treatment.

» If you are having thoughts of wanting to die or of hurting yourself or someone else, you should contact your doctor right away.

Causes and Contributing Factors

Like postpartum depression, postpartum anxiety has several causes that can contribute to symptoms developing. These may include a personal history of depression, anxiety, substance use disorders, or a personal history of traumatic experiences. Other factors that may increase the risk of postpartum anxiety include relationship strain or instability, lack of social support, financial strain, employment stress, unplanned pregnancy, teen pregnancy, or pregnancy complications such as hyperemesis, previous miscarriages, fertility challenges, or medical complications with the baby.

In the postpartum period, factors that lead to depression in some women may lead to anxiety in others: hormonal changes (for example, when restarting birth control or stopping breastfeeding), a difficult or traumatic birth, premature delivery, a baby in the NICU, a baby with health complications, having twins/multiples, breastfeeding difficulties, a baby with a difficult temperament, or a high-needs older child at home. Emotional factors, such as anxiety about baby care, sleep deprivation, feeling a loss of control, or struggles with one's sense of identity can also contribute to depression and anxiety.

As discussed in the chapter on depression, breastfeeding challenges can increase a parent's anxiety level. Feeding your child, whether via breast or bottle, should be a nurturing and pleasant experience for both baby and parent. If breastfeeding and/or pumping is a contributing factor for a mother to feel great distress or anxiety, it's okay to consider adjusting the feeding/nursing plan. If you are experiencing breastfeeding challenges, seek out skilled lactation care. If they don't address the issues you bring up, or tell you to "just keep doing what you're doing," and don't listen to your concerns, talk to someone else to get your needs met.

Misunderstandings about Postpartum Anxiety

» **I don't have postpartum anxiety. Isn't being anxious all the time just part of being a parent?**

We have heard this exact question many times, and the answer is no. Being a parent should not cause you to feel anxious all the time. There are stressful, anxiety-provoking parts of parenting, especially for first-time parents with a newborn. However, that sense of tension, worry, or fear shouldn't be there most of the time. It is common to suddenly realize that your baby has taken a longer nap than normal and hurry into the room to make sure they are still breathing. Most parents have this experience of momentary anxiety. They check on the baby, and all is well. It is more concerning when a parent checks on a baby 5 to 10 times per night when the baby is not awake or crying.

» **I have frequent intrusive thoughts about harm coming to my baby. This must mean that I could actually hurt him.**

Having distressing thoughts pop into your mind unexpectedly is a common symptom of postpartum depression and anxiety. In the vast majority of cases, the parent is not at risk of harming the baby, and in fact, they usually feel terrible about even having the thoughts. Having some intrusive thoughts is pretty common. This happens because we don't want anything bad to happen to our baby. However, when these thoughts are frequent and repetitive, and the parent can't push them aside or recognize them as irrational, then they should reach out to their healthcare professional.

» **I'm stressed, but I don't need to ask for help – I just need to go to yoga and take some deep breaths.**

Yoga and deep breathing can certainly be helpful for stress and anxiety, *and* if you are experiencing many of the symptoms we described earlier in this chapter, then these may not be enough to help you feel better over the long haul. There are many things that can help reduce anxiety but telling yourself to "just breathe" minimizes the larger experience that you're having. When deep breathing isn't enough, anxious feelings build up over time. The exercise and meditative aspects of yoga can be a great stress reliever, but if someone is experiencing daily anxiety, yoga should not be their only tool, but one part of a larger plan to feel better.

» **I don't feel depressed, so I'm fine. This stress will pass on its own.**

A common misunderstanding is that the only mental health issue that someone can experience after a baby is born is postpartum depression. This ignores the very real, intense anxiety many parents experience. Postpartum depression often comes with some anxiety, but postpartum anxiety does not always include depression symptoms. When we assume depression is the only possibility, parents may suffer from anxiety in silence because it is misidentified as the normal stress of caring for a baby.

Sometimes anxiety will remit on its own, but when it doesn't, and if it lasts for weeks or more and is present most days, then it's essential to get help.

PARENTS and Postpartum Anxiety

Let's apply the PARENTS acronym to postpartum anxiety for some approaches to managing these symptoms.

 Practice Patience

More important than positive thinking is practicing patience with yourself. There are so many social pressures on parents today; it's easy to fall into a perfectionistic thinking pattern. So many parents feel and think that they have to make every decision perfectly for their children, never get mad or frustrated, read several books a day to their child to develop their mind, expose them to music, art, tumbling, and swim classes. These imagined standards are impossible to achieve, and as a result, parents can fall into a trap of toxic social comparison and critical internal self-talk.

We encourage parents to practice patience and balanced thinking about themselves, their children, and their parenting. On any given parenting day, whether you have small children or teenagers, there are highlights and lowlights. Though it's good to think about the not-so-great moments and what could have gone better, it can be even more important to reflect on the uplifting parts of the day too. Focusing on the sweet, proud, loving, or silly moments helps balance your thinking. Having a balanced perspective helps you feel less guilty, less flawed, and gets you closer to feeling that you can be a good enough parent. One way to keep perspective is to take 5 minutes at the end of each day to write down 3 positive things that happened that day. Over time, you'll end up with a long list of these highlights. Later, when feeling down or stressed, you can refer back to this list to help recalibrate.

Two other effective anxiety-reduction techniques are Square Breath and 5 Senses. Square Breath is simple and more effective than just taking deep breaths because it helps you avoid shallow, anxious breathing patterns and more effectively regulates breathing.

» Start by inhaling for a count of 4. Then hold it for a count of 4. Exhale for 4 counts and then hold for a count of 4. Repeat 8 to 10 times.

The second skill, the 5 Senses (Linehan, 2014), is a grounding technique that helps refocus your attention away from anxious thoughts.

» The first step is to pick one of the five senses (sight, hearing, taste, touch, or smell). We suggest first trying sight because most people find it easiest. The parent describes everything they see around them in as much detail as they can. A key aspect of this exercise is the level of detail. The specific item being described doesn't matter, but by focusing on the details of the object, chair, tree, office, laundry room, the brain is forced to use non-emotional aspects of cognition that help to interrupt the cycle of anxious thoughts. This same exercise can be done similarly with other senses. For example, take a bite of your sandwich and describe in as much detail as you can the taste, texture, and smell of that bite.

Activities for Yourself

Try some low-intensity activities to reduce stress. Consider starting a daily meditation practice – it can be short, even a brief 5 to 10 minutes per day. Several meditation and mindfulness apps are available for smartphones and tablets; many are available for no cost. These are a great place to start because they will help guide a novice in simple, easy-to-follow steps.

R **Rest and Sleep**

Getting adequate sleep is important to regulate our moods day to day. It's even more important when someone is experiencing anxiety. There are many strategies that can be used to relax and lower anxiety. However, most of them require some mental bandwidth - that is, having enough emotional energy to engage in these stress-reducing behaviors. A helpful technique that doesn't require so much energy is called Serial 5s (Beaudoin, 2014).

> » While comfortably lying in bed, in a dark room, pick a song, poem, prayer, etc. Anything simple that you have memorized. With your eyes closed, you will say each word 5 times

before moving on to the next word and so on. For example, using Twinkle, Twinkle Little Star, you would say to yourself, *"twinkle, twinkle, twinkle, twinkle, twinkle, little, little, little, little, little, star, star, star, star, star"* and so on.

Like the 5 Senses technique, repeating each word 5 times gives your mind something else to focus on, quieting the anxious thoughts. Many people also find the rhythm soothing, helping them to physically relax and fall asleep.

 Exercise and Movement

Exercise is a well-documented mood enhancer. It can be uplifting when you're down and can be calming when you're feeling on edge. To get the mental health benefits, you need only exercise 2 to 3 times a week for 20 to 30 minutes at a moderate pace (Mayo Clinic, 2021). Yoga is just one example of an exercise that can be particularly helpful for parents who are struggling with anxiety because it requires you to slow down and be mindful of your breath and body. A studio yoga practice is a great way to socialize while you exercise, but at-home practice is a good option too. There are many beginner and intermediate classes available for free online. These may be ideal for a parent with multiple kids at home or for someone who doesn't have the time or financial resources to join a studio or gym. If yoga isn't for you, that's ok because there are lots of other great ways to get exercise. Find any physical activity that you enjoy and make the most of it.

 Nutrition

There are many books available about nutrition, and the effects food can have on our mental health. For purposes of this topic, a specific piece of advice for those struggling with anxiety is to be cautious with caffeine. Caffeine is stimulating and taking in too much can mimic symptoms of anxiety. Water, of course, is best but if you like to drink something with a little flavor, consider flavored waters or decaffeinated teas, sodas, or coffee. If you need a little pick-me-up in the morning, try half-caffeinated, half-decaffeinated coffee. Pay close attention to how you feel afterward as even lower levels of caffeine can make an anxious person feel more on edge.

T Time with Others

Spending time with supportive loved ones and friends is a great natural anxiety reducer. Talking with a best friend or sharing a fun activity with a sibling allows us to take a break from our daily routine and demands. Spending time with other parents and sharing stories and challenges can reassure us that we're not alone in our struggles. Many cities have parents groups in which you can get to know others in your area and expand your social circle. Parenting, especially for stay-at-home moms and dads, has the potential to feel isolating. Joining a group is a great way to connect with others.

Another option that we frequently recommend is signing up for an Early Childhood and Family Education (ECFE) class. These classes are usually run through your local school district. They are generally affordable, and some may even have scholarship/partial payment options. The classes are based on the child's age and families can start when their children are as young as newborns. We like these because parents get to meet other people with children the same age, and the classes have a focus on education and understanding child development.

Support Network

Anxiety may be triggered by feeling overwhelmed with too many things to do or feeling inadequate to accomplish the tasks at hand. Using your social support system is essential. Friends and family can help with simple things like running errands, helping with housework, or childcare so that you can get a break to engage in hobbies, take a nap, or run errands without kids in tow. We often work with moms and dads who believe that they are supposed to have it all and do it all, all the time. These are unrealistic expectations. It's impossible to be on your A-game all day, every day. It helps to step back from these expectations, accept that no one is perfect, and ask for help. Your anxiety and stress will lessen, and you'll be able to enjoy your life, family, and children because you won't always be thinking about the next thing to complete and where you're going to find the time to do it.

An easy way to stay connected with friends is to have an ongoing online connection (think group texts, online chats, video exchanges) with some of your closest friends. Babies and toddlers can be time-consuming, so having free time to talk on the phone or go to lunch can feel impossible. Connecting online is faster, and it can reach several people at once. Sometimes in those hard parenting moments, we just need to vent or get some reassurance that we're doing okay and that others have had that struggle too.

Revisiting Krystal

Given Krystal's anxiety, she started therapy with a cognitive-behavioral focus. Over several sessions, she worked on increasing her awareness of emotional triggers and cognitive patterns. Krystal learned how to recognize these patterns more readily and challenge the irrational thinking she was engaging in before it could intensify her anxiety. A theme that arose was her strong tendency to want to fix everything and the anxiety she felt when that was not possible. In therapy, she discussed ways to let go of this unrealistic expectation. One strategy was scheduling a time for Krystal to worry. It may sound like a funny idea, but it can be an effective way to control how much you worry. In her case, she would schedule (she even put it in her calendar) a daily 30-minute time slot. During that time, she would give herself permission to worry as much as she wanted about whatever she wanted. But when the 30 minutes was up, she had to stop. This is one of the cognitive-behavioral skills that helped her gain a sense of mastery over her anxious thoughts.

Another source of stress for Krystal was the behavior of her husband's ex-wife. She looked for ways in which she could more effectively navigate and set boundaries in this relationship. Additionally, Krystal learned new communication skills that she could use when talking to her husband about his ex-wife's behavior. This helped Krystal and her husband feel more like a team in co-parenting and helped Krystal establish a place in the lives of her stepkids. She found a local stepmoms' group that meets monthly. This group became invaluable to Krystal, helping her better understand the challenges she faced with co-parenting. It also normalized her frustrations with her husband's ex-wife; knowing that she wasn't the only one with these struggles was reassuring.

Eventually, Krystal decided that she also wanted to try an antidepressant medication. It wasn't robustly helpful at first, but after a few dose adjustments, the medication was effective. With the benefit of medication to reduce some of her anxiety symptoms, Krystal found that *she was even better able to use the skills she learned in therapy.*

Revisiting Jaclyn

Since Jaclyn had previous experience with therapy, she was able to pick up where she left off. Cognitive-behavioral therapy had been effective for her in the past, so she and her therapist revisited that approach. With this pregnancy and postpartum, she found herself engaging in a frequent cycle of negative self-talk and unrealistic expectations about her mothering abilities. Her perceived inability to meet these self-imposed standards was causing her great anxiety and self-doubt. She learned to challenge these thoughts with more accurate data and reflect on her experiences, rather than having purely emotional responses like, "I feel like I'm failing, so I must be a failure."

Jaclyn began engaging in repetitive behaviors like repeatedly reorganizing her kitchen pantry and counting her frozen breast milk supply. It was in reflecting on these behavioral symptoms that she got to the heart of what was really causing her anxiety – her feelings of being out of control - and organizing was a way to feel more stable. She practiced using her adaptive emotion management skills to address the real roots of her anxiety, which in turn, helped her reduce the compulsive behaviors.

She also addressed the catastrophic thoughts and "what-if" scenarios she was feeling about bringing her daughter to daycare for the first time. While still on maternity leave, Jaclyn was able to arrange a practice day with her daycare provider. This practice was more to benefit Jaclyn than the baby, but it was enough to help her push past the anxiety she was feeling, and she coped well when the real daycare drop off day came, and she had her first day back at work.

This course of therapy lasted about 3 months. During that time, she also worked with her psychiatrist. They did not adjust her antidepressant medications, but about halfway through her maternity leave, they did opt to add an as-needed anxiety medication for moments of particularly acute symptoms. With the medications and therapy, Jaclyn's transition back to work was smooth, and she was better able to cope with the demands of being a working mom of two young children.

CHAPTER 8

ANTEPARTUM AND POSTPARTUM ANXIETY IN THEIR OWN WORDS

As with postpartum depression, we wanted to bring you the thoughts and words of real people who have experienced anxiety during pregnancy and the postpartum period. Let's hear from the two moms you read about in Chapter 7.

Krystal

Were there times you didn't feel like your usual self? What were those times like? How did you know something was different?

The red flag that I was not myself was the thoughts that turned dark so frequently. It wasn't like I was suicidal, but as I was gardening, a bus would be coming down the street, and I would have a fleeting thought that it would be easier if I just walked in front of the bus, and it could all stop.

While I struggled with challenges with my older stepchildren at home, I would be driving my toddler and baby and start to think about the best place to move to start life over on our own. It was like having someone else's voice in my head. It was frightening. I had problems with anxiety turning to panic. Thoughts would get stuck on repeat, and I didn't have the tools to make them stop. Until I got help, the worry and darkness felt louder and louder.

When did you know that you needed to ask for help? Who did you go to first? What did that person do or say that was helpful?

When I struggled with worry that played on repeat, I first talked to my best friend, who had also struggled with anxiety and understood panic. She knew me in my younger days when I had panic symptoms, and she helped reassure me that I had gotten my anxiety under control before, and I would be able to do it again. Most importantly, she just listened.

I also talked with my husband as soon as I had thought patterns I did not recognize. He has struggled with chronic depression since he was a teen and assured me that a depressed brain can play awful tricks and make you believe reality looks darker than it is.

What did you find was most helpful for starting to feel better?

Due to a previous difficult birth, I had located mental health help while I was still pregnant. I did not want to carry my anxiety to term with my baby. I started with a healing birth trauma group and then found a therapist to work through my anxiety. When my thoughts turned darker after my son was born, I was able to start working with that same therapist on those patterns and get an appointment with a psychiatrist who prescribed medication, safe for use in breastfeeding, that put me back in a mental state where, with the help of my therapist, I was able to work through challenges more effectively.

Did you see a therapist? What was psycho-therapy like? How was it helpful?

Seeing a therapist was very helpful to me. In addition to my struggle with postpartum depression and anxiety, I was a mom to 2 kids and stepmom to 3 other children. Having someone help me sort out my new responsibilities allowed me to figure out how to be a good parent to all 5 of them while I was healing and rebuilding healthier thought patterns.

Did you take medication(s)? Did you have hesitations about taking medication? If so, what were they? What was it like to take medication(s)? How did the medication(s) help you feel better?

When my thoughts started drifting to driving off bridges and jumping in front of buses, even though I didn't really want to die, I knew there was something happening in my brain that I didn't want to become a pattern. I was hesitant to start medication while still nursing my son but finding a psychiatrist who took my hesitation seriously and talked me through the risks and benefits so I could weigh my decision with better information was helpful. I found benefit immediately from the medication – probably because I was taking control of my problem rather than letting it take me away from my life and my joy. Beyond the initial boost of controlling my own health, I found that the darker thoughts started to fade and I felt more like myself.

What advice would you give to parents who are experiencing mental health difficulties after their baby is born?

If you know someone who has struggled with anxiety or depression, reach out to them for support. It's a difficult mindset to understand unless you've lived it.

Are there other things you would like to share about your experience with anxiety during your pregnancy and postpartum anxiety?

When seeking professional help, remember it takes time. I've found the first couple visits with a new mental health practitioner can aggravate my anxiety, like sharing the problem with someone you don't fully trust yet, gives it extra weight. That initial struggle is worth it though, when I found someone who was a good match and helped guide me out of the fog of anxiety and depression.

Jaclyn

Were there times you didn't feel like your usual self? What were those times like? How did you know something was different?

After experiencing late-onset postpartum depression and anxiety with my first pregnancy, I was acutely aware that my second pregnancy felt different. I latched onto any pain and any fear, and it consumed me. Though my pregnancy was planned, it occurred at a time when our family was dealing with the cancer diagnosis and treatment of my father-in-law. After my pregnancy was confirmed at home, I needed several blood tests to monitor the hormone levels in my blood and was told that my pregnancy was most likely a chemical pregnancy and may not be viable. I was concerned that my husband would not be able to support me through the pregnancy, especially at the beginning, due to his father's recent diagnosis. However, I also felt like he would be upset if I didn't tell him about the pregnancy right away and then went through a miscarriage. I felt on edge in a way that I didn't during my first pregnancy, so I knew something was not right.

When did you know that you needed to ask for help? Who did you go to first? What did that person do or say that was helpful?

When I was diagnosed with gestational diabetes, I latched onto a comment made by a health-care professional who said I was "high-risk times three" due to my age (35), my weight, and my gestational diabetes diagnosis.

After that, I became even more anxious about everything to do with my pregnancy and being certain that I would not be able to carry the baby to term. I thought, "I should have tried harder to lose weight. I should have gotten pregnant sooner after my first child was born so I wasn't considered advanced maternal age." Everything felt like my doing, my fault. I was failing this baby before it even existed.

My husband began to tread lightly around my anxiety, casually mentioning the therapist I had seen after my first child was born. He gently encouraged me in the direction of seeking therapy and reminding me about my experiences with my first pregnancy with depression and anxiety.

Did you see a therapist? What was psychotherapy like? How was it helpful?

Towards the end of my second trimester, I called to make an appointment with the therapist I had seen previously. She had availability on her calendar, and I began seeing her weekly. It was helpful to re-engage with someone who knew my history of postpartum depression/anxiety. She was able to remind me of things I had said during my first round of therapy, and over time, this helped me to better contextualize my current emotions and fears.

Did you take medication(s)? Did you hesitate about taking medication? If so, what were they? What was it like to take medication(s)? How did the medication(s) help you feel better?

My therapist encouraged me to see a psychiatrist. The conversation around changing medications or adding medications during my pregnancy was terrifying to me. I felt that the odds were already so stacked against the viability of this pregnancy that changing anything chemically seemed too risky.

During my first meeting with the psychiatrist, she took the time to understand my first pregnancy treatment plan, how I felt before my second pregnancy and how I felt currently. She described some of the chemical and hormonal things that happen during pregnancy and how medications could help.

What advice would you give to parents who are experiencing mental health difficulties after their baby is born?

My advice to parents who are experiencing mental health difficulties after their baby is born is to be open with their partner or any other supportive person in their life about how you are feeling – someone who knows you, even if they haven't been a parent or experienced mental health challenges. They can help you understand the differences in your mood during and after pregnancy, and since they know you, they'll be able to compare that to moods prior to your pregnancy.

I don't have a lot of friends, but I am still learning to rely on the supportive people that I have in my life beyond my partner. This helps lighten the burden on him so he's not my sole support person.

Are there other things you would like to share about your experience with anxiety during your pregnancy and postpartum anxiety?

Postpartum depression is not just the baby blues and often takes a new mom a while to identify. My experience with postpartum depression started pretty early postpartum but then hit really hard after I stopped nursing/pumping at nearly a year. It was difficult for me to recognize this as postpartum depression since my son was almost a year old.

My journey in treating my postpartum mental health put me on a path to bettering my whole self. I have learned a lot about why I am the way I am and continue to learn to this day. I still fight my anxiety in my role as a parent, but I am better equipped with tools. Medication helps my brain see clearly enough to understand the realities of anxiety, and therapy gives me the education and tools to navigate through the hard times.

CHAPTER 9

DEPRESSION AND ANXIETY IN DADS AND OTHER PARENTS

Patient Story - James

James was thrilled when he found out his partner of 4 years was pregnant with their first child. They had been trying for a pregnancy for about 10 months, and he was happy when the long wait was finally over. The pregnancy went well, but labor was long, and unfortunately, there were medical complications during delivery. This was a scary experience for James and his partner because things seemed to move really fast once they were at the hospital. Thankfully, the doctors and nurses who cared for them were able to sit down with James and his partner after the birth and review what had happened, which was reassuring.

Despite that, for weeks after the birth, James would feel anxious when he thought of the delivery and his fear that something bad might happen to his partner or the baby even now. He slept poorly as a result, and it didn't help his sleep to have a baby who was pretty fussy and hard to soothe. He worried a lot about the safety of his newly expanded family. After a few weeks, he started to feel down and a lot more irritable. He stopped his usual habit of running twice a week. He found it hard to enjoy his fantasy football league, even though this was usually a highlight of his week. When he was around the baby, he didn't feel connected to his son and worried that he wasn't as skilled at baby care as his partner or the baby's grandparents. He started to avoid being alone with the baby, which led to him feeling even less confident as a father. He didn't feel like a "real man" and asked, "how can I be a real man if I can't take care of my family?" He wasn't eating much and lost a few pounds. He couldn't stay focused at work and feared he'd lose his job as an accountant as a result of making some errors on a major client's portfolio.

Emotional Distress in Non-Birth Parents: The Basics

One in 10 new fathers will suffer from Paternal Postnatal Depression (PPND), and 18% will develop an anxiety disorder (Postpartum Support International, 2021). There's a common misconception that perinatal mood and anxiety disorders are all about hormones. While shifts in hormone levels probably do play a role in these conditions for birth mothers, that's not the only cause. Sleep deprivation is a stressor for anyone. Relationship strain appears for some couples when parenting isn't exactly what they expected. We know that issues like these can be risk factors for developing PMADs. In fact, when moms have postpartum depression, there is about a 50% chance that dad will develop depression symptoms as well (Paulson & Bazemore, 2010).

Trying to learn about and effectively respond to a newborn's needs is no easy task. Balancing the wishes of family and friends, trying to maintain a healthy romantic relationship with a co-parent, and keeping up with work and other activities are all highly demanding when there's a newborn in the picture. These stressors can, for some, lead to symptoms of depression and anxiety. The good news is that these conditions can respond well to treatment, whether that's psychotherapy, medications, or self-care strategies like the PARENTS method.

We recognize that the second parent in a family may not be a dad. It may be another mom, or the secondary parent may be a grandparent or other family member. Adoptive and foster parents are also among those considered in this chapter. Because there are so many possibilities related to who might experience these symptoms, for the remainder of this chapter we've decided not to use the common term *paternal postnatal depression* but instead *postnatal depression or anxiety.*

Typical Symptoms of Postnatal Depression and Anxiety

Increased anger and conflict with others

» A quick temper and angry reactions may be more intense than the situation calls for. Frequently, these irritable feelings can lead to conflict with family, friends, coworkers, or even strangers, which then adds another layer of distress.

Feeling easily overwhelmed

» This may happen even in the context of relatively minor problems or stressors. Parents may feel unable to cope when multiple things are thrown at them at once, often leading to emotional reactions that seem out of proportion to the situation. Others react by shutting down and disengaging emotionally.

Worry that is present most the time and is difficult to control

» Anxiety may be hard to "turn off," and it can feel like you can't escape the worries. This often has the effect of leading the person to feel on edge, not in control of their life, overwhelmed, and agitated.

New or increased use of alcohol or other drugs

» People often turn to alcohol and drugs to numb or escape uncomfortable feelings. Occasional alcohol use may be fine, but it becomes a problem if drinking is heavy or frequent. If a parent or others have concerns about someone's alcohol or drug use, that's often a red flag indicating that there may be something else at the root of the substance use.

Frustration or irritability

» Frequently parents who are struggling after bringing home a new baby feel on edge or like they could blow up at any moment. This is often mislabeled as an anger management problem when the true cause is really depression and/or anxiety.

Panic attacks

» Panic attacks are characterized by intense anxiety for a short time that may occur out of the blue. They usually come with physical symptoms like racing heartbeat, sweating, shortness of breath, and dizziness. Sometimes people have the feeling that they're going to die or "go crazy."

Violent impulses or outbursts

» These are often related to the increased anger and irritability that a parent may be feeling. Frequently, being unable to control outbursts is a sign that someone's emotions are on the edge, and they are likely feeling overwhelmed.

Changes in appetite and changes in weight

» Anxiety and depression commonly affect appetite or interest in food. Some people find they lose their appetite, and others may overeat to try to comfort themselves. When this is severe or persistent, people may lose or gain noticeable weight.

Isolation from family and friends

» It is common for someone experiencing depression and anxiety to isolate themselves from their loved ones. A typical experience described by people struggling with depression is feeling like they have to fake being okay or "put on a mask" of happiness. As a result, socializing can feel draining or unappealing when a person is not feeling well.

Ruminative worry

» This type of worry feels like it's on a loop in your mind. Often, people find themselves worrying about the same topics over and over again with great difficulty stopping the thinking pattern. The mental exhaustion that comes from this cyclical thinking is a contributing factor to irritability and emotional outbursts.

Intrusive thoughts

» Intrusive thoughts pop into our minds unexpectedly and are usually unwanted and distressing. Sometimes they are fleeting, lasting just a few moments. Other times, they repeat over and over. They may include negative thoughts about how someone perceives themselves, stressful life situations, or the world at large. A common theme of such thoughts is fears about the health or safety of the family.

Feeling discouraged

» If part of the experience of parenting is feeling inadequate or not living up to self-imposed or cultural expectations, it is easy to feel discouraged. Raising a child feels like one of the most important things someone will do in their lifetime. So if you feel incompetent about something so meaningful, it's not a stretch that you'd start thinking negatively about yourself and your parenting abilities.

Physical symptoms

» Physical symptoms like headaches, stomach problems, and pain are common in both anxiety and depression. There is a strong connection between our physical health and our mental health. People don't always recognize this connection and then mislabel these physical symptoms as unrelated to their emotional experience, which leads them to choose fixes that don't make them feel any better in the long run.

Problems with concentration and motivation

» Depression and anxiety often cause a person's thinking to feel foggy or unclear. Being easily distracted or forgetful is common. Low motivation or lack of interest in things is a hallmark of depression.

Loss of interest in work, hobbies, and intimacy

» Depression usually leads people to have trouble enjoying the things that would normally be pleasant for them. This may, in turn, worsen depression because these positive outlets no longer feel as helpful in relieving distress.

Working more or spending more time outside of the home to avoid family life

» If a parent feels incompetent caring for a new baby, it's natural that they may throw themselves into work or outside activities that allow them to feel accomplished and therefore, feel better about themselves. It is normal to need breaks from the stress of childcare, but if a parent is consistently avoiding the family, it can lead to interpersonal problems with their co-parent and/or child.

Fatigue

» Depression and anxiety can sap a person's energy. This can be compounded by not sleeping well, which can be caused by the depressed feeling itself and by a child who isn't yet sleeping consistently at night.

Conflicted feelings about what it means to be a man, woman, mother, father, or parent

» Becoming a parent means that we are faced with changes to our identity, and this transition can be difficult to navigate. It is normal to have conflicted feelings about these major changes; what these new labels mean to you and if you feel you are meeting cultural and societal expectations of the new role.

Thoughts of suicide

»   When depression is significant, people sometimes have thoughts of not wanting to be around, wanting to escape their life situation, or even of wanting to die. If these thoughts are happening, it's important to reach out to family or friends and to a trusted medical professional.

When to Reach Out to Your Healthcare Professional

Everyone has a bad day or a bad week sometimes, and it is normal to experience some of the symptoms described above some of the time. Bringing home a new baby is stressful and changes nearly all aspects of your life. Experiencing several of these symptoms for many days might mean that depression or anxiety needs to be evaluated and addressed.

Remember, if you have some of these symptoms, check in with a trusted support person, whether a family member or friend or a professional. If you have thoughts of suicide or of harming others, you should reach out for support right away. A good place to start is to call your primary care doctor. Most places around the United States have suicide hotlines or crisis support phonelines. You can also reach out to local mental health resources. If your thoughts are feeling particularly scary, you can always call 911 or go to your local emergency room. It's vitally important not to ignore these symptoms. You can feel better!

Causes and Contributing Factors

Dads, same-gender non-birth parents, adoptive parents, foster parents, stepparents, grandparents who are primary caregivers: there are lots of people who are parents, or function as parents, to a newborn. They all have some risk of depression and anxiety symptoms coming on in the early stages of baby care. This makes sense given that parenting a newborn leads to major changes in lifestyle, day-to-day activities, expectations, and sense of self. All parents may struggle, even if they weren't the one who carried the pregnancy or gave birth.

The field of mental health care is learning more and more about the experiences of non-birth parents and how their mental health is affected by various stressors. One thing that we often see in our practice is "maternal gatekeeping." This occurs when the mom (or whoever is the primary caregiver) does *everything* for the baby – every diaper change, every feeding, every bath, every bedtime. Often, the person doing this feels great about how well they are doing as a parent, but this has an unintended consequence of keeping the other parent out of the baby's life. The second parent doesn't get one-on-one time or the opportunity to practice parenting skills with their son or daughter. With first-time parents, this can be particularly stressful for the non-birth parent who may be less comfortable with many baby-care skills. This feeling of disconnection from the baby or incompetence as a caregiver can lead to depression and anxiety. We recommend that new parents do their best to share baby duties from the beginning. This benefits both parents and the baby, who then gets to know and feel comfortable in the hands of each of his/her caregivers.

Another contributing factor to depression and anxiety symptoms is the social pressure dads may feel as they craft their own definition of what it means to be a father. Dads have to navigate expectations from the more traditional past and the evolving present. They may have been socialized to be the "man of the house" and a breadwinner. And now they may also be expected to be much more actively involved in childrearing and household duties. This can lead to feeling like there isn't enough energy or time to be successful in all these roles, leading to self-doubt, and if that becomes severe, to depression and anxiety symptoms.

Patient Story - Kim

Susie and Kim met in college and had been in a relationship since their mid-twenties. They got married in their early 30s. Soon after, they started to plan for a family. Susie decided to carry the pregnancy, which was conceived via IVF and sperm donation from an anonymous do-nor. The pregnancy went well, although she did have mild gestational diabetes, so she had to be vigilant about what she ate in the later part of pregnancy. Their daughter was born on a snowy day in January. The baby was not too fussy and slept pretty well, even from an early age. However, Susie had trouble with breastfeeding due to low milk supply and trouble with the baby's latch that never really seemed to improve. She'd always envisioned breastfeeding for at least a year, and she felt guilty about not being able to meet the expectation she'd set for herself. She started to feel more down and sad and sometimes was kept awake at night by worries about the baby's health.

Kim felt frustrated and often irritated, as though there was nothing she could do to help her wife feel better. It seemed that Susie was pushing her away, and their relationship was strained. Kim also felt like she was never given the opportunity to be alone with the baby because Susie was so afraid for the baby's health and safety. As a result, Kim felt less able to soothe the baby, and every time their daughter would cry, Kim would feel highly anxious – she'd feel sweaty and shaky, her heart would race, and sometimes she'd feel like she might pass out. Susie was hesitant to seek help for herself, which made Kim's feelings of frustration even worse. She didn't have many social connections other than Susie, and eventually, she started to consider leaving the relationship. Everything seemed so bleak and hopeless, she wasn't sure things would ever get better.

Misunderstandings about Postnatal Depression and Anxiety

» **Only moms can get depressed after the birth of a baby.**

Having a newborn requires a big adjustment in priorities and expectations for what life will look like, now and for years to come. Anyone caring for a newborn, not just a birth mom, can develop symptoms of depression or anxiety because caring for a baby can be stressful even under the best of circumstances. If issues arise like breastfeeding difficulties, a baby who's not a sound sleeper, job stressors, or any number of other concerns, those can compound the already demanding adjustment to parenting. All caregivers are vulnerable to developing these symptoms. The good news is that these symptoms can get better once they're addressed.

» **Postpartum depression is caused by hormones, so dads/non-birth parents can't get it.**

Hormones are probably one factor in the development of depression or anxiety symptoms after a baby is born, but they're certainly not the only factor. Changes in hormone levels, and the ways those changes affect mental health, are not completely defined yet. Some women may be more sensitive to shifts in hormone levels that accompany pregnancy, delivery, and postpartum, *and* there are many women for whom those hormone shifts don't seem to cause any trouble. Other factors play a role too when people develop symptoms of depression or anxiety: humans are well known to have trouble adjusting to change, and having a baby is one of the biggest changes there is in life.

» **If you are sad and anxious, you should just "man up". It will go away on its own.**

Some sadness and worry are normal in the postpartum period – after all, this is a new experience for most everybody. If the sadness and worry don't last long and don't get in the way of day-to-day life, it's possible they may just resolve on their own. However, for many people, these don't resolve, and they do get in the way of day-to-day activities. That's when getting help is important. Without addressing these concerns, they're likely to get worse and can interfere with parenting, relationships, and work. To prevent that from happening, getting help might take the form of therapy or medications, and usually also involves a focus on self-care and stress reduction: the PARENTS method can be helpful with that.

PARENTS and Postnatal Depression and Anxiety in Non-Birth Parents

Let's apply the PARENTS method for some approaches to managing the symptoms of postnatal depression and anxiety for non-birth parents.

 Practice Patience

Nobody is an expert parent from the beginning. You can read all the parenting books and blogs you like, but until you start the on-the-job training phase of parenting, you really can't predict how it's going to go. Give yourself a break if things don't go as anticipated and be flexible with your expectations to avoid disappointments. Some things are bound to go well, even wonderfully, but some things won't, and that's okay. Every parent struggles at times, some more than others. If you love your child and stay focused on that, you're already on the right track.

Activities for Yourself

What did you do for fun before the baby was born? Try to keep doing it. Even if you can't do it as well, or as often, keep at it. Physical activity can be especially helpful because you get the benefits of exercise as well, so if you're a runner or golfer or basketball player, stay on track with those activities. If you're a reader, keep reading, even if you can only cobble together an hour per week to read. If you're a cook or a foodie, keep trying new recipes and restaurants. It's easy to let things slide when you have a new baby at home, and you may not be able to do as much as you used to, but try to fit a few fun things into each week.

 Rest and Sleep

Finding time to rest, much less truly sleep, is a tall order when you've just brought a baby home. It goes without saying that when you have an opportunity to sleep, you should take it, especially in the first few weeks with a new baby. Once your child starts sleeping on a more predictable schedule, sleep will get easier for you too, but until then, it's catch-as-catch-can. Aim for at least 6 hours total, over 24 hours, if you can get it. That may mean you and your partner take shifts sleeping or trade-off nights to be on baby duty. While this approach would be tough on a relationship if you were planning to do it for the next 18 years, if it's only for a few weeks or months, then your relationship can weather it. Most importantly, if you both get about the same amount of rest, there won't be a lopsidedness to who's feeling exhausted.

Exercise and Movement

Two hours of daily high-intensity cross-training at the gym is unnecessary, and you don't need to start training for a marathon to see mental health benefits from exercise. That's probably not possible anyway if you've got a newborn to take care of, on top of all your other obligations. There's plenty of research confirming that exercise is a potent antidepressant and antianxiety strategy, but you don't need to go to excess to feel better. To get the mood benefits, the general recommendation is to exercise 2 to 3 times a week at a moderate intensity (Mayo Clinic, 2021). Getting out for a brisk walk, taking a bike ride, playing a sport with friends, doing an online workout session, or going rock climbing are a few ideas. Find an activity that's fun for you and run with it (pun intended).

 Nutrition

There's no secret diet that improves mental health, but we know that eating well can make a difference. What does a healthy diet consist of? Advice may vary depending on whom you ask, but most people with expertise in the field will agree on a few basics. It makes sense to avoid heavily processed foods and stick with whole foods, including fruits and vegetables that are as close to their natural form as possible, lean proteins (poultry, fish, legumes), and healthy fats. Avoiding excess sugar (which is found in *many* foods and in some surprising places, so be sure to read nutrition labels) and avoiding highly processed carbohydrates is a sound approach. Eating a variety of different foods will help maintain vitamin and mineral levels to keep you healthy, and this will help with mental health as well as physical well-being. It's also prudent to minimize and monitor alcohol use. It often happens that people drink more, and more frequently, during times of high stress.

A simple and effective strategy is to make several dinners with extra portions on the weekend to eat over the course of the next few days. Having premade, nutritious, and tasty meals makes dinner time after a long day of work and childcare much easier.

T Time with Others

Plan date nights. It's hard to fit these into all the baby care, work demands, and household management that has to happen, but it's worthwhile to make time to spend as a couple. Put a date on the calendar at least once or twice a month. It doesn't have to be anything extraordinary: a movie and dinner is just fine, a fun Netflix binge after the kids are asleep, even a walk around the park without kids in tow can feel refreshing. We highly recommend doing "day dates"; finding childcare for a few hours is often easier and tired parents usually have more energy during the day rather than at night, when getting to bed early might be the best decision.

S Support Network

Don't lose touch with your family and friend support network. They can help make this transition time easier. It can be particularly helpful to check in with friends and family who have kids of their own; they usually have great advice and can offer lots of reassurance about the normal experiences of parenthood. Their advice may keep you from having to reinvent the wheel when it comes to your own family routines and having someone's ear to bend can be an excellent stress-reliever. Support people can also be helpful in lightening your workload – if you've got someone who can do some projects around the house, run errands on your behalf, or babysit for date night, ask them for that support. People want to help out, and if the roles were reversed, you know you'd be happy to step up for them.

Revisiting James

James had a colleague at work who was supportive (and was a new dad himself). He noticed that James didn't seem like himself and suggested reaching out to his primary care doctor for help. James did contact his doctor, who offered to refer him to a therapist and to start a medication for anxiety and depression symptoms. James felt like therapy wasn't really his style, but he did elect to start a medication, and after a few weeks, things started to turn around. He felt less irritable and anxious. His sleep also improved because he was less anxious at night. He started to feel like "the old James" again and noticed he was more resilient in the face of the stressors in his life. Those stressors hadn't gone away, but he wasn't so overwhelmed by them and could cope better. James felt more comfortable being more involved in childcare, and this practice helped him gain the confidence that he needed. He also found himself with more motivation to get back into activities like his fantasy football league and regular exercise.

Revisiting Kim

Kim loved her wife and didn't want to leave the relationship. She decided to contact a therapist she had seen a couple of years earlier. Kim saw her for therapy on her own, and for some sessions, Susie would join her so they could work on their marriage too. Kim worked with this therapist for several months. Much of what they focused on was the negative self-talk she was engaging in about her parenting skills. She also developed skills so that she and Susie could more effectively communicate, and Kim learned how to be more assertive about asking to help with the baby. In the end, both parents were able to settle into their new roles and feel good about the state of their marriage.

CHAPTER 10

TRAUMATIC EXPERIENCES IN PREGNANCY AND CHILDBIRTH

Patient Story - Brianna

Brianna was pregnant with her first child. They knew it was a boy, and she and her partner were ecstatic about having their baby. Her pregnancy went smoothly, and she felt good for most of it until the later weeks of her third trimester, when, like many women, she began to feel uncomfortable and have difficulty sleeping. She went into labor at 40 weeks, 2 days gestation. Labor progressed uneventfully, and Brianna felt she was managing the pain okay, but after about 12 hours, labor stopped progressing. After another

2 hours, her doctor became worried about the baby's heart rate, which was dropping significantly with each contraction.

Another doctor and two nurses rushed into Brianna's hospital room. The medical staff were talking amongst themselves. The new doctor abruptly turned to Brianna's partner and told him that they would need to do an emergency cesarean section. The nurses prepped Brianna for surgery and within moments, they were wheeling her down the hallway to the operating room; Brianna's baby was born just a few minutes later. The baby was healthy, and Brianna didn't suffer any additional medical complications herself, but she couldn't shake the feeling that her birth experience wasn't what she wanted or had envisioned.

For months, Brianna would replay the birth over and over in her mind, thinking about how she could have avoided a cesarean section, even though her OB reassured her there was nothing Briana could have done differently. Sometimes these thoughts popped into her mind unexpectedly, and she would have a hard time concentrating on the task she was doing. She also felt angry at times and recalled feeling extremely fearful when the medical team *rushed her into the operating room. She felt like things had spiraled out of control, and she was afraid that her baby would die at delivery. This fear led her to check on her infant son several times per night to make sure he was still breathing. Brianna had no previous history of mental health concerns or traumatic experiences. The feelings she was having were overwhelming, leading her to feel anxious and sad most days. She would often feel guilty for having these feelings because "everything turned out fine. I'm fine. The baby is fine."*

Pregnancy Trauma and Traumatic Childbirth: The Basics

The DSM-5 (Diagnostic and Statistical Manual 5th edition) is the book published by the American Psychiatric Association that defines conditions like depression, anxiety, and posttraumatic stress disorder (PTSD). According to DSM-5, formal diagnosis of PTSD requires that someone has A) experienced a trauma and B) had specific psychological and/or physical symptoms after that trauma. A trauma is defined as a situation in which the person was exposed to actual or threatened death, actual or threatened serious injury, or actual or threatened sexual violence. The person may have experienced the trauma themselves or may have witnessed it happening to someone else. The symptoms that someone might experience after the trauma include things like psychological distress, flashbacks, insomnia and nightmares, avoiding things that remind them of the trauma, among several others. Those symptoms are described in more detail, with examples, in the section below entitled "Typical Symptoms of Trauma."

A distressingly large number of mothers experience childbirth-related trauma. Over 30% of women have a traumatic birth experience with at least some symptoms of PTSD, even though they may not meet formal criteria for the diagnosis (Beck, Driscoll, & Watson, 2013). Approximately 9% of women will meet the full formal diagnostic criteria for PTSD following childbirth (Postpartum Support International, 2021).

It can be difficult to recognize childbirth trauma, and that can lead to a parent's concerns being dismissed. Sometimes it feels hard to believe that a birth would be considered traumatic if mom and baby are physically healthy after delivery. Parents may wonder why they have PTSD symptoms if "everybody is ok now." But birth trauma is real regardless of the outcome of labor or childbirth.

Cheryl Beck, a renowned researcher in birth trauma, described traumatic childbirth as "an event occurring during the labor and delivery process that involved actual or threatened serious injury or death to the mother or her infant. The birthing woman experiences intense fear, helplessness, loss of control, and horror" (Beck, 2004, p. 28). This definition is useful because it highlights the mother's *experience*, and not the outcome, as foundationally important to how the trauma is defined. Many women who go through a traumatic birth have heard comments, whether from friends, family, or clinicians, along the lines of "everything is okay because you and the baby are okay." Though the outcome is important, of course – we want mom and baby to be safe and healthy – the mother's experience of the birth is even more important. Beck coined the phrase "trauma is in the eye of the beholder" to illustrate this point. It's not about what the medical team thinks or what her spouse or others think; it's the woman's experience of the event that determines whether it was traumatic. If a parent or partner felt that their life or health was in danger, or if they felt the baby was in danger, that trauma is *real*.

It's also important to consider the experiences of the other people in the delivery room. The DSM-5 definition above highlights the idea that trauma is experienced when there is a threat of death, injury, or sexual violence. A birthing woman's support team (spouse, family member, best friend, or whoever may have been present) witnesses the birth, and they, too, could have a trauma reaction from a frightening situation. Research on fathers exposed to birth trauma suggests that those who experience PTSD symptoms have difficulty asking for help and may tend to cope through avoidance and escapism (Etheridge & Slade, 2017). So, when a complicated or scary birth occurs, it's important for all involved to be mindful of their reactions and mental health.

Sometimes there is an objectively bad outcome related to pregnancy. This could be miscarriage, stillbirth, or injury to the mother or baby at delivery, for example. Parents and families will understandably feel traumatized when things don't go right, and grief under these circumstances can be particularly acute and painful. These parents are also at risk of developing symptoms of PTSD and should have a low threshold for seeking professional support in the wake of an injury or loss.

Typical Symptoms of Trauma

Mothers who've experienced birth trauma may have some or all of the symptoms listed below. Friends and family who were in the labor room may also experience these symptoms:

Intrusive distressing memories, thoughts, or dreams about the birth

» Intrusive thoughts are distressing thoughts that pop into our minds, possibly triggered by a specific stimulus (a smell, sound, thought, image, etc.). With pregnancy and childbirth trauma, women may find themselves replaying the whole birth experience or specific aspects of the birth over and over in their minds, analyzing every detail of the event to figure out what happened or what went wrong.

» Flashbacks are the feeling of reliving the traumatic experience. They can be intense and scary. Sometimes people get lost in their experience of the flashback, so much so that they seem to temporarily disconnect from the outside world. This is referred to as "dissociation."

» Nightmares are common after a traumatic experience. They can be vivid, sometimes disturbing, and likely disrupt sleep patterns and restfulness.

Avoidance

» Once someone has experienced a trauma, it is common for them to avoid places, people, smells, sounds, or other stimuli that remind them of the traumatic experience. Excessive avoidance may get in the way of them living their usual lifestyle.

Feeling detached or estranged from others

» After trauma, people frequently isolate themselves from friends, family, or the world at large. This can increase a person's sense of loneliness and sometimes leads to depression. After a traumatic experience, people might feel a sense of detachment that they describe as being "on autopilot" or feeling "like a zombie," as though they're just going through the motions of life and not feeling entirely present in the moment.

Inability to remember important aspects of the event

» This is a common experience for people who have experienced trauma. MRI studies show that the trauma-exposed mind will automatically "shut down" parts of the brain as a protective measure (Samuelson, 2011). This shutting down process impairs how memories are stored, which creates gaps. If aspects of an event never register in the parts of the brain that store information, there will be no way to recall them later.

Thoughts that lead the person to blame themselves or others for the event

» Many people who have experienced trauma feel as though there was something that they could or should have done differently to prevent it from happening. Or they may feel someone else could or should have done something differently to prevent the negative experience. Sometimes those feelings are justified by the circumstances of the trauma, and it may be true that things could have gone differently. For others, the trauma can distort perceptions of what could realistically have been done differently. This can lead to doubts and rumination, and excessive feelings of guilt.

Irritable behavior and unprovoked anger outbursts

» Many people who have experienced trauma have strong anger reactions or intense irritability. Typically, these reactions feel out of proportion to what the situation calls for, and the person may feel as though they have little control over their reaction.

Hypervigilance

» Hypervigilance is the experience of being on alert for danger or triggers that could lead a person to be reminded of a traumatic event. This may lead people to feel tense, emotionally on edge, and anxious.

Exaggerated startle response

» Because people often feel the effects of trauma in physical ways, being on edge most of the time and feeling easily startled is a common experience.

Sleep disturbance

» This refers to chronically disrupted sleep, not just a hard night or a bad week. The inability to fall asleep or stay asleep is common, and people may wake in the middle of the night with intrusive memories or thoughts of the traumatic experience.

When to Reach Out to Your Healthcare Professional

If you have experienced trauma related to pregnancy or birth, consider seeking professional help. This may come in a number of forms: sometimes sitting down with the doctor who delivered your baby and reviewing the events with them can provide perspective on the situation. If that's not helpful, it may make sense to seek out a therapist or psychiatrist to help you process your experience. They can help with evaluating your symptoms and recommending treatment options. Other widely-available resources can be helpful in navigating trauma and PTSD; for example, the National Center for PTSD has self-assessment tools and information on recovering from trauma.

If you feel you can't keep up with your usual obligations at work, at home, or interpersonally, consider getting help and support; this might be with a mental health professional, through a peer, or via a support group. If you have thoughts of suicide or of harming others, it's imperative that you seek help from a qualified professional. Those kinds of thoughts may not go away on their own if you don't seek help, but they can be resolved if you get timely mental health care.

Causes and Contributing Factors

Many of the contributing factors to depression and anxiety symptoms that were reviewed in earlier chapters may contribute to the development of PTSD symptoms. Additionally, there are some factors that are specific to traumatic pregnancy and childbirth.

A previous history of PTSD or exposure to traumatic events can be a risk factor for further trauma. Women who have experienced a previous trauma, such as sexual abuse/assault or a prior complicated birth, are at higher risk for experiencing postpartum PTSD (Postpartum Support International, 2021). Birth complications such as an unplanned cesarean section, postpartum hemorrhage, perineal trauma, and others, may raise a mother's risk of PTSD. Having a baby who needs to stay in the NICU or Special Care Nursery raises PTSD risk for parents as well. Parents who felt powerless as the birth was occurring or as procedures were being done may be more vulnerable to the lingering effects of trauma. Some women who describe their birth as traumatic say that they experienced limited or inadequate communication with doctors and nurses at the time of the traumatic experience. A strong predictor of birth trauma in recent studies was the mother's relationship with her providers (Simpson, 2015). If the care was harsh or insensitive, she was more likely to experience trauma.

Socioeconomic factors may also play a role in PTSD risk. Intimate partner violence in the context of pregnancy difficulties layers one trauma upon another. Poverty, racism, and community violence are among other stressors that may predispose parents to have persistent posttraumatic stress symptoms.

Patient Story - Marisol

Marisol was a recent immigrant to the Upper Midwest from Ecuador. A marketing professional back home, she had struggled to find sustained employment in her field after moving to the U.S. with her 6-year-old daughter. Adjusting to her new country was difficult without extended family around to provide support. She didn't have much time to spend with the few new friends she met, and finances were a strain. After about a year in the U.S., she met her boyfriend, Jared. She was surprised by an unexpected pregnancy after they had been dating for only 4 months. During the pregnancy, Jared grew more and more unkind - he would yell at her or call her names, and do the same with her daughter. Without other supports nearby, she couldn't find a way to leave the relationship. He became more abusive and eventually shoved her into a wall when she was about 34 weeks along. She started to have contractions after that and worried she'd lose the baby. She sought help from a domestic violence support organization and was able to find temporary shelter housing, and ended up delivering her son at 36 weeks. He was in the Special Care Nursery for a week after his birth for additional medical monitoring. During that time, she had nightmares about Jared pushing her and couldn't sleep well. Driving by the hospital would leave her anxious, with a racing heart and tremors, so she would avoid the area when she had to run errands or take *her daughter to school. She missed some of her son's pediatrician appointments because she couldn't stand the sounds and smells of the medical clinic. When she started working, she found it difficult to focus and concentrate - she was distracted by her thoughts of Jared, and the baby's hospital stay.*

Misunderstandings about Traumatic Childbirth

» **Since the baby and I are okay, I just need to get over these feelings I'm having.**

People often tell themselves this after they've had a challenging or traumatic childbirth. They may also hear this message from their friends, family, or even medical professionals. It's wonderful that you and baby are doing okay physically but as we've talked about in this chapter, *how* you experienced your birth is important. If you're feeling upset or confused about what happened, that's okay. You should not try to suppress or ignore these emotions.

» **PTSD is something that soldiers experience, not moms. I'm just being too sensitive about how my birth went.**

It's common to think of a soldier when you first hear "PTSD," but trauma and PTSD are not just caused by combat. Trauma can be caused by many types of events and experiences. Any event in which your or someone else's safety is at risk can trigger these symptoms. If you felt scared or fearful during your birth, it's understandable to have post-traumatic stress symptoms afterward. You're not being overly sensitive, dramatic, or weak.

» **My birth was complicated, but I'm okay, so I'm sure my spouse feels okay about it too.**

Possibly, but sometimes loved ones who witness a birth can have upsetting experiences. We've had patients with complicated births who feel okay about what happened, but their partner, who was in the delivery room, developed PTSD because of the fear they felt when the complications were occurring.

» **If I feel my birth experience was traumatic, it means that I'm a weak person and that I did something wrong while in labor.**

Having a traumatic experience or PTSD has nothing to do with someone's strength of character. Trauma symptoms are physiological and psychological reactions to a life-threatening event; reactions that are outside of the person's control because they happen automatically as your brain attempted to protect you. It's natural to think you could have done something to prevent a bad thing from occurring or to look for a reason or cause for an event. In the most challenging births, there are multiple factors that may contribute to complications. The trauma symptoms you're experiencing are not your fault.

» **I'm so upset about how my birth happened. I'll never be able to have another baby.**

After a traumatic or scary labor and delivery, many women feel this way. With the right support and, if necessary, mental health treatment, you can come to feel differently. You may choose not to have another baby, but you, not your fear, will be in control of that decision.

PARENTS and Trauma

Let's apply the PARENTS method to managing symptoms of trauma during pregnancy and childbirth.

 Practice Patience

One helpful mindfulness skill is called the 5 Senses (Linehan, 2014), which we also reviewed in the chapter on postpartum anxiety. Trauma can cause you to feel distracted or disconnected, and this skill can help ground you in the present moment. Start by choosing one of your 5 senses: sight, touch, hearing, taste, or smell. We recommend starting with sight because it tends to be the easiest for most people. In this case, start to describe what you see, either out loud or in your head, in as much detail as you can. Don't rush; focus on the details. You can describe what you see in the room, what you see through the window, the pattern of the blanket your baby is wrapped in, and so on. This skill works by using the frontal cortex of your brain, which is the area in charge of more complicated processing, as opposed to the more primitive emotion-generating parts of your brain, which cause the negative feelings of PTSD. Most people find that they only need to do this technique for 30 to 60 seconds before they feel more grounded. This can be repeated with the same sense or another of the five senses, as often as is helpful.

 Activities for Yourself

After a traumatic or complicated birth, it can be helpful to talk to your doctor about what happened. If possible, this can be done in the hospital shortly after delivery, but often, a woman may not realize that she is upset or confused about her birth until several days or weeks later. If you find yourself replaying parts of the birth over and over in your head or feeling angry, anxious, or confused about why a medical intervention occurred, we recommend that you make an appointment with your OB or midwife to go over the birth events with you. This can help fill in gaps in your memory, and the doctor can explain why certain medical interventions were recommended. Having an understanding of what happened and why can reduce distress about the trauma.

Rest and Sleep

As we've noted in previous chapters, sleep and rest are important for mood and mental well-being. Traumatic experiences can most definitely affect sleep, so it is important to get sufficient rest. It can be a challenge to find time to sleep, but this is when it can be essential to ask for help. Consider asking a grandparent, friend, or trusted neighbor to come over to watch the baby while you nap. It's even better if they can come and help for an overnight. Bad dreams can be a consequence of traumatic experiences, so if your sleep is persistently disrupted by night-mares, racing thoughts, and anxiety, consider reaching out to a healthcare professional to help get you back on track.

E **Exercise and Movement**

Since many people experience trauma in their bodies, physical activity can be a great way to minimize those sensations and feel more in control of your body. Once you are medically cleared by your doctor, consider trying moderate exercise. We often recommend yoga, as it can be a gentle way to resume an exercise routine and has a strong emphasis on being mindful of your body and breath. Other options to consider would be a group exercise class with a close friend, weight training, or even something as simple as going for a walk over your lunch hour. The goal is to engage your muscles and your cardiovascular system.

 Nutrition

Because anxiety symptoms are commonly a part of traumatic experiences, limit caffeine, which can cause sensations that mimic anxiety. We also recommend limiting alcohol use. Alcohol can lead to behavioral disinhibition, which can be particularly destabilizing for someone who is feeling the psychological and physical symptoms of trauma. Don't use alcohol to self-medicate distressing feelings because it can lead to problematic long-term consequences. Alcohol can also worsen depression and anxiety symptoms. Other substances of abuse can lead to equally troubling consequences for physical and emotional health.

T Time with Others

After a traumatic event, many people's natural inclination is to isolate themselves, so they don't have to talk about or think about what happened. Though some time alone can be healthy for everyone, consistently avoiding friends and family can ultimately make you feel worse. Consider focusing your social time on your most trusted friends and family. When you do spend time with them, don't hesitate to set boundaries around topics that you may not feel ready to talk about. Sometimes the best medicine that loved ones can provide for us is a safe, comforting space to do things, like watch a funny movie, talk about what's going on in others' lives, enjoy a meal together, or take a walk outdoors. These simple activities, in a relaxed environment, can be just the mental break that you need.

S Support Network

After anything challenging or scary, connecting with trusted friends and loved ones can be helpful. With traumatic childbirth, it can also be helpful to talk to other women who have had similar experiences so that you know that you are not alone. You could look for a local or online support group. For some women, hearing other people's stories may trigger their own posttraumatic symptoms, so it will be important to make these types of connections when you feel ready. This can be a different experience for different women, so don't be afraid to find a support group and consider attending on a trial basis for a session or two. If it doesn't work for you, move on to something that does.

Revisiting Brianna

Brianna experienced many of the symptoms described earlier in this chapter, though she was never formally diagnosed with PTSD. Brianna tried to hold these feelings in for many months. At her son's 6-month pediatrician appointment, she filled out an EPDS, a screening questionnaire for depression and anxiety. She'd completed an EPDS several times before, at the pediatrician's clinic and her OB's office, but now for the first time, she answered honestly because she recognized she wasn't her "usual self." This particular EPDS score helped her son's doctor have a more meaningful conversation with Brianna. She accepted a referral to see a therapist. After meeting the therapist for the first time, she learned more about what she was experiencing and how common traumatic childbirth is. In therapy, Brianna processed her birth experience to help her cope with the memories that were causing her anxiety symptoms. She learned skills to counteract her negative self-talk about feeling that her body "failed her" in childbirth. She also learned practical anxiety-management skills to use when she felt overwhelmed. Brianna was in twice-monthly therapy for about 6 months. She did not take a daily medication for her symptoms but did periodically use a medication to help her sleep when her anxiety led to insomnia.

Brianna's story is common, and therapy can be effective for these types of symptoms. Two years later, when Brianna was pregnant with her second child, she returned to therapy. Though she was generally doing well, she noticed herself feeling anxious about the upcoming birth. This second round of therapy focused on reinforcing the skills she learned before and helping her create a birth plan to boost her confidence with this delivery. She and her partner also discussed how he would advocate for her and their preferences if she were unable to. Brianna attempted a vaginal delivery, but in the end, she had another cesarean section. However, this time around, she felt like an active participant in the decision *making and as a result, her second postpartum experience went much better.*

Revisiting Marisol

The domestic abuse support organization that Marisol had previously worked with was able to help her connect with resources for mental health care. The psychiatrist's office had a care coordinator who found emergency housing funds for a few months and a job coach. The job coach connected her to some marketing agencies, and through Marisol's networking around the metro area, she was able to find another job with a steady income in her chosen field.

She also discussed treatment options with her psychiatrist. She expressed interest in a therapy group based on cognitive-behavioral therapy (CBT) approaches (see more on CBT in chapter 12). She attended the group for 12 weeks and learned valuable skills for managing anxiety and for viewing her traumatic experiences through a new lens that made them feel less threatening. She also elected to start medication for PTSD. The first one she tried led to some nuisance side effects, so she switched, and the second medication worked well for her, with no side effects. She started to sleep through the night most nights, her concentration and focus improved, and she felt less anxious about going to her medical appointments. With her stress and anxiety levels lower, she found she started to enjoy time with her children, and she sought out new socialization opportunities through work and with other parents from her daughter's school. She even joined a running club and started to train for a 5K.

CHAPTER 11

THE PARENTS METHOD WORKSHEET

Now that you've read through the PARENTS sections of the previous chapters, let's put the ideas into action. Below, you'll see a simple chart we've created to get you brainstorming various ways to feel better. You don't have to fill in every box in every column, but we encourage you to consider as many as feasible to build your repertoire of strategies.

Here's an example of how to use this worksheet: maybe you feel like the postpartum depression chapter described your experience best. Start by rereading the PARENTS section for that chapter. Choose a few strategies that stand out for you or something you haven't previously considered but would like to try. List those in the worksheet below to help remember your ideas and solidify your approach. You don't have to limit yourself to the ideas in that chapter. Though we tailored the PARENTS suggestions to each concern, many of them can apply to other experiences, so it may also help to go through the other chapters and consider any of those self-care strategies as well.

Though it may feel time-consuming to write things down, it helps to think ahead and make things concrete. This will also assist in keeping you accountable to trying these approaches. Writing down ideas (on paper or electronically) can give you something to easily refer back to later, since it can be hard to think of helpful ideas when you're feeling sad, anxious, or overwhelmed. You probably won't need to use this worksheet forever as these skills will eventually become automatic once you've practiced them enough, but we encourage you to try it for at least a few weeks. It may help to jot notes to yourself about what was helpful or not when you tried the strategy.

Finally, don't be shy about trying something new or something you hadn't thought would work for you. Our patients sometimes feel awkward at first when we make some of these recommendations, and it's normal to feel nervous about something new if you feel like you're out of your comfort zone. If you can push past that uneasiness, we think you'll discover strategies that are effective for you and your new family.

	Week of:	Week of:	Week of:	Week of:
P Practice Patience				
A Activities for Yourself				
R Rest and Sleep				
E Exercise or Movement				
N Nutrition				
T Time with Others				
S Support Network				

CHAPTER 12

TREATMENT OPTIONS

While there are many ways that new parents struggle with the transition to having a new baby at home, the good news is that for parents who have depression or anxiety, there are treatment options available. Many things can help parents to feel well again and to feel like things are back to normal and more manageable. Research has illuminated the many routes to mental wellness. When it comes to managing depression and anxiety symptoms, treatment plans should be customized to the individual. The answers for one person may be entirely different than for another. Fortunately, a wide variety of approaches can all be successful. A treatment plan needs to make sense for the individual and the family, and whatever approach is chosen must fit into their own specific life circumstances.

There are many ways to get help. Any number of professionals who care for new parents and their families can be enlisted to start the process of getting symptoms treated: psychologist, psychiatrist, OB/GYN or midwife, pediatrician, primary care doctor, visiting home nurse, doula, or lactation consultant, among others. Any of these clinicians should be aware of resources for struggling parents, and many can start some form of treatment directly. There are also national and international organizations that are dedicated to helping new parents with mental health concerns. One such organization is Postpartum Support International. They offer many resources for parents, training in perinatal mental health for clinicians, and a comprehensive list of qualified perinatal mental health clinicians around the world.

In the sections below, we focus on the use of medications and psychotherapy as treatment options for perinatal mental health concerns. Naturally, there are other approaches, but these are two that have consistently been shown to be effective. While we do most of our work with medications and therapy in our practices, we also know the value of approaches like the PARENTS method for a holistic care plan.

Medication

There are several medications available to treat depression and anxiety symptoms. New studies are always being published, and updated information can change how psychiatrists think about the safety of those medications in pregnancy or breastfeeding. Because specific recommendations about medications can change, in this book we don't offer suggestions about particular medications or doses.

It's reassuring to know that many medications used to treat anxiety and depression can be used safely in pregnancy and breastfeeding. Parents can research medications with a reputable source such as Thomas Hale's book *Medications and Mothers' Milk*, the Massachusetts General Hospital Center for Women's Mental Health, MotherToBaby (mothertobaby.org), the InfantRisk Center (www.infantrisk.org), or LactMed, the National Library of Medicine's Drugs and Lactation Database (https://www.ncbi.nlm.nih.gov/sites/books/NBK501922/). Because databases like these can provide up-to-date evidence-based information, but can't provide individualized treatment recommendations, we also strongly encourage consultation with a psychiatrist who has expertise in using medications in pregnant and nursing patients.

There is a common misconception that people should avoid taking any medications during pregnancy because they may be harmful to the baby. A few decades ago, the public health world started to look more closely at potentially toxic exposures in pregnancy. Overall, that was a good thing because, for example, most people now understand that things like alcohol and tobacco can be problematic in pregnancy or breastfeeding. It may be, however, that that public health message got a little too much traction, so that many people mistakenly believe that *any* exposure to *anything* during pregnancy or breastfeeding is toxic. Thankfully, this is not the case.

An important consideration for psychiatrists seeing pregnant or nursing patients is the balance of risk and benefit when it comes to treating psychiatric symptoms during pregnancy or breastfeeding. Consider a non-psychiatric example: if a mother were diagnosed with diabetes (diabetes is chronically high blood sugar and the complications that result) years before pregnancy and has kept her blood sugars stable by using one of the usual medications to manage diabetes, such as insulin, we would advise her to keep using insulin during her pregnancy. We know that if she stopped using it, she'd be at risk for higher blood sugars, which can lead to things like damage to blood vessels, kidney disease, vision problems, and pregnancy complications. Even if the medication posed some risks to the baby when taken while pregnant, we'd still recommend that she continue to take it because, on balance, the risks to her and to her baby are too high if she stopped taking it.

The situation is similar with psychiatric medications. We know from research over many decades that untreated depression or anxiety can have negative effects on mothers and on their babies. There is the obvious concern that mothers with untreated depression and anxiety are suffering emotionally, or the medication would not have been prescribed in the first place. We also know that untreated psychiatric symptoms can lead to problems with the baby's development physically, emotionally, and cognitively. Luckily, there has been much research examining the safety of medications for depression and anxiety in pregnancy and breastfeeding, so we have hundreds of studies to guide prescribing. This volume of research tells us that many of the medications we use are appropriate for pregnancy and breastfeeding, and in most cases, the benefit of treating a mother's depression and anxiety symptoms far outweighs the (low) risks of medication exposure. Making a connection with a psychiatrist experienced in caring for pregnant and postpartum people can be invaluable for getting accurate information about medications and about the risks of not addressing psychological symptoms.

See the reference list at the end of the book for selected research studies related to the safety of psychiatric medications in pregnancy and lactation.

Misunderstandings about Medication

» **Medications will make me feel like a zombie.**

This is a common concern, but fortunately, it's not a common experience with medications for depression and anxiety. Medications should not make you feel flat, unemotional, zombie-like, or feel as though your personality has changed. If that's your experience, it means you're probably not on the right medication for you, and you should see your doctor about making changes. Usually, we recognize that medications are effective when parents come to see us and report that they "feel like themselves again." Parents also often say they feel "back to normal" or that they're more resilient in the face of stressors. That's the goal of treatment with medications.

» **Once I start, I'll have to take medication for the rest of my life.**

While some parents do decide to take medications on a long-term basis, we often recommend that once a person is feeling better, they continue taking the medication for several months before stopping it, because the risk of symptoms returning is lower than if they stop taking it sooner than that. Many parents are able to stop the medication at that point and remain well. However, some parents come to feel so much better with medication treatment that they elect to continue taking the medication for a longer period of time. This is something you and your doctor can discuss and plan together.

» **Medications are addictive.**

Some psychiatric medications do carry a risk for dependence, but the majority of medications that are first-line treatments for anxiety and depression do not have this risk. People who have struggled with addiction previously may be more likely to struggle with certain medications, especially some of the medications that are used on an as-needed basis for anxiety. You should always be forthcoming in sharing any past struggles with addiction with your doctors so that they can choose medications that will be appropriate and safe for you.

» **It's dangerous to take medications during pregnancy or breastfeeding.**

As noted above, many of the medications we use to treat anxiety or depression can be used safely in pregnancy and breastfeeding. You'll want to connect with a psychiatrist, obstetrician, or primary care doctor who is up-to-date on the latest research about psychiatric medications to help with decision-making and treatment planning.

» **It's selfish to take medications during pregnancy or breastfeeding.**

The healthiest thing for a baby, whether in utero, in infancy, or in later childhood, is having a healthy parent. If you're not well, it will be harder for you to be an effective and loving caregiver, and that has negative consequences down the road for you *and* your child. When you're calm, content, and well-rested, you'll be a better parent. Healthy parents make for healthy kids.

Psychotherapy

There are many misconceptions about psychotherapy, and these can lead people to feel anxious about going or to avoid it altogether. This may be rooted in how the media tends to portray therapy. Most therapists you've seen on TV or in the movies are a pretty inaccurate portrayal of the profession. It seems that in many big- or small-screen representations of therapists, within a few minutes of arriving on the scene, the therapist does something so unorthodox or unethical that they would lose their license in real life. It makes for an entertaining show but is nothing like what real therapy is like.

Most everyone is nervous during a first therapy session – it's hard to tell a stranger what's bothering you or how you are struggling. A good therapist will help you feel comfortable, despite that nervousness. Decades of research have shown that the effectiveness of therapy is in large part due to the quality of the relationship between the patient and the clinician (Norcross & Wampold, 2019). This develops over time, but many patients feel the beginnings of that connection early on. That also means if, after several appointments, you don't feel that connection, it's okay to look for someone new.

Psychotherapy is a combination of exploring current and past experiences, sharing with a trusted and safe person, and learning new skills and strategies to better cope with your life stressors. There is no one way to do it and no cookie-cutter format that works for everyone. As the therapist gets to know you, they will learn the most effective ways to help and what skills will be beneficial to you. It is often held that therapy is a *process* – it has to unfold over time. Even though it may not be an immediate fix, therapy with new parents who are struggling with depression and anxiety can be effective, and many people start to feel some relief and improvement after just a handful of sessions.

For decades, researchers have studied what types of therapy are most effective. For perinatal mood and anxiety disorders, the two most research-supported treatments are:

» Cognitive Behavioral Therapy (CBT): This type of therapy focuses on recognizing and challenging negative and irrational thinking patterns.

» Interpersonal Therapy (IPT): This type of therapy focuses on improving interpersonal relationships, role transitions, and communication.

There are additional types of psychotherapy that may be helpful for learning to cope with past traumatic events and traumatic childbirth, such as Eye Movement Desensitization and Reprocessing (EMDR), sensorimotor therapy, or Accelerated Resolution Therapy (ART). These work by having the patient gain more mastery over distressing memories or events. Many patients find the skills from Dialectical Behavioral Therapy (DBT) to be useful. DBT has a focus on building specific and practical skills in 4 areas: mindfulness, interpersonal effectiveness, emotion regulation, and distress tolerance.

Most psychotherapists consider themselves "integrated" therapists, meaning that they integrate aspects of several types of psychotherapy to address their patient's unique concerns. The therapies listed in this chapter are a small sampling of the options available. It is welcome and encouraged that you ask a potential therapist about their style and what types of therapy models they use most often.

Many people who have never had experience with mental health care wonder what therapy will be like. In the first session, the therapist will ask you a variety of questions so that they can begin to get a sense of what's going on in your life that brings you to therapy. For new parents struggling with anxiety and depression symptoms, the therapist may also ask about:

» When and how the baby was born, to understand how long the symptoms have been present and how you experienced the birth

» Your daily mood

» Your support system and how easy it is to access it

» Your experience with breastfeeding or bottle-feeding and whether there have been any unexpected challenges

» The baby's health

» How you've been doing with daily activities outside of taking care of the baby (showering, cleaning, cooking, errands, working, etc.)

» What your sleep patterns have been like, and whether you are able to fall asleep when you have the opportunity

» Any feelings of being overwhelmed, help-less, or hopeless

» Your appetite

» Thoughts of hurting yourself, someone else, or the baby

» Violence or abuse in interpersonal relation-ships

Some of the themes that commonly arise in therapy for perinatal mood and anxiety con-cerns include:

» Changing identities and role transitions

» Feeling overwhelmed and incapable

» Frustration with a partner who isn't helping as much as the other parent expects

» Feeling guilty about asking for help

» Social isolation

> » Worries about making the "wrong" decisions for the baby

> » Anxieties about a chaotic or traumatic birth experience

> » Concerns about feeling sad/anxious again (if there was postpartum depression or anxiety after a previous birth)

One way to gauge whether therapy might be helpful is to ask, "how am I coping?" Notice that the question is not "how am I doing?" which leads most of us to answer "fine" out of habit or social expectation, even when we're not fine. That's why "how am I coping?" is a better question. It leads you to consider a deeper question about your experience – not just that you're getting by and getting the basics done – but rather, how it feels to be functioning the way you are. If your answer is something like "terrible," "not great," or "it could be better," then psychotherapy can be a great option, since a main goal is to increase coping abilities with new skills and strategies.

Misunderstandings about Psychotherapy

» **Therapy takes forever to work. I don't have time for that.**

If consistent with appointments, most people start to feel better pretty quickly, depending on how bad they were feeling when they started therapy and what the treatment goals are. Since the early stages of therapy for perinatal depression and anxiety tend to focus on practical skills, most people start to feel better as soon as they start to use these skills.

» **You have to go to therapy multiple times a week for it to be effective.**

Most people go to therapy once a week or once every other week in the beginning. As you start to feel better, it's common to space the appointments further apart.

» **Therapy is all about talking about your childhood, and I don't want to do that.**

Therapy with new parents tends to be practical and solution-focused, with an emphasis on the present and how to more effectively manage emotions and the negative thinking someone might be engaging in. However, sometimes it can be useful to talk about your early life experiences, as this assists you in better understanding why you may be reacting to stressors the way you are now. Many parents find that thinking back on how their parents raised them can be helpful, either in order to repeat what their parents did well or to avoid things that they did less well.

» **Therapy is just paying someone to listen to you and "be your friend." I have lots of friends that I can talk to for free.**

This is a common misconception about therapy. Your therapist actually should not be your friend, but of course, they will be *friendly*. There are lots of ways that a therapy relationship is different from a friendship; many of these are laid out in professional ethics codes and have the purpose of protecting the patient by keeping the relationship appropriate. An objective opinion from someone who isn't in your family or social circle can give new or different perspectives to help you see things from a different angle. Unlike most of your friends, a psychotherapist has trained for years in human psychology and behavior and should be up-to-date on the research about the most effective ways to treat mental health conditions. In other words, a good therapist will do more than just listen. Their knowledge and expertise will help you learn new coping strategies, better understand unhelpful relationship patterns, and figure out how to communicate more effectively.

Involving Loved Ones in Appointments and Decisions

Though you want your treatment plan to be personalized to your needs, it can be helpful to have loved ones (spouse, parent, sibling, friend, etc.) involved. If these important people are aware of your treatment plan, they can support you with those goals. Of course, it's best to include those who will truly be supportive and will not undermine your decisions.

It is not uncommon for partners or loved ones to come to the initial appointment with a mental health professional. They likely have questions and could have some of the same misconceptions about depression, anxiety, and the various treatments. In order for them to be supportive, it's ideal for them to accurately understand what psychotherapy entails or to understand the beneficial effects and potential side effects of a medication. When one parent is struggling with depression and anxiety, it affects the whole family unit, so it makes sense to include all the essential support people from that family.

CHAPTER 13

PREPARING FOR FUTURE PREGNANCIES

It can be scary to think about another pregnancy if you've had struggles with depression or anxiety during or after a previous pregnancy. Fortunately, every pregnancy is different, so if you had a rough time after your first baby was born, it doesn't mean that the same will be true when your second is born. Many people have a better experience with a subsequent pregnancy. You'll know better what to expect and having that understanding can be helpful. However, it may not be totally safe to just assume that it will be easier, so it makes sense to set up some strategies to increase the likelihood of a better postpartum period. It's important to think ahead of time about how to make future pregnancies go more smoothly.

The strategies in the PARENTS method can be useful for addressing concerns that are happening now and for preventing difficulties in the future.

In the next chapter, we present a Postpartum Plan worksheet that lists some of the concerns that tend to present themselves after bringing home a new baby. These are topics and themes that can be sources of conflict or distress for new or experienced parents. We encourage you to review the worksheet not only for first pregnancies but for later pregnancies as well. If you're a parent who has been through pregnancy and postpartum already, you've gained special insights into how the postpartum period works, what it's like to care for a newborn, and how your life changes with a baby. That experience will help you think about the topics in the worksheet. If you are pregnant now and have not yet brought your baby home, talk to friends and family about the topics on the worksheet. They will have plenty to share about their experiences. This information can help you think through how you might react to upcoming changes or what supports you might need.

A few things stand out when planning future pregnancies. One of those is working to develop insight into the difficulties of a past pregnancy/ postpartum period and learning from those struggles. The other is planning ahead for the future. You'll want to make sure that you have a reliable team of supports in place. That support network might include a significant other, extended family such as your own parents or parents-in-law, friends, and backup childcare providers.

If you have the option, look for an OB/GYN, midwife, or pediatrician who is tuned into the mental health needs of new parents. A crucial part of building the team can be finding (or continuing to see) mental health clinicians such as a therapist and psychiatrist. Ideally, these clinicians would have lots of experience in treating people during and after pregnancy. If you want to find vetted mental health clinicians, one helpful resource is Postpartum Support International's website (www.postpartum.net). They have lists of clinicians with expertise in perinatal mood and anxiety concerns, organized by state, province, and country.

How can someone gain insight into past events, experiences, and struggles? One way to do that is through psychotherapy. Exploring what went well and what didn't, especially if it's done in the setting of psychotherapy, can be invaluable in making the future different from the past. A therapist can help to process whatever was stressful or challenging and can guide your exploration into the reasons for those challenges. A better understanding of that means you can be vigilant about seeing similar signs or patterns in the future. When you're watching for these signs and ready for them, you're better equipped to manage or even eliminate negative experiences that may result.

We're aware that there are many parts of the United States and around the world where access to high-quality mental health care, including effective psychotherapy, is limited. If internet access is available, online therapies can be useful. This can take the form of one-to-one video conferencing ("telemedicine") or manual-based, more general-purpose approaches. If mental health services are limited, it may be necessary to build a support network that mainly includes non-professionals, like family or friends. There are also many online support communities. When it comes to online support, especially social media forums, caution is important – for basic safety, but also regarding the unfiltered nature, and sometimes inaccuracy, of the information that may be posted. Having a sense of healthy skepticism is key to managing expectations.

Connecting with other parents can also be an option to review past experiences and challenges, for example, through playgroups, your children's school, your faith community, or other family-oriented events. For more ideas, look back to our previous chapters and under "Time with Others" and "Support Network" in the PARENTS method sections. If you're able to find a way to connect with other parents who've had mental health concerns in the context of pregnancy and postpartum, all the better, because there's great comfort in being understood by people who "get it."

Communities like the ones just described can also be helpful in building your future support network. Having support around mental health concerns, in particular, can make for a sound safety net. Assistance with daily life, such as household management, balancing work and children, and maintaining a solid relationship with a significant other are things to try to arrange ahead of time. Child care assistance is especially important to have in place before the baby comes. Friends or family can be great resources for this, assuming they're available, willing, and able to help out. If they're not available and you have the means, backup childcare help can come from a nanny or babysitter. Even the friendly teenager down the street can allow parents to have a few hours of respite, so they're good to have on the roster of helpers too.

When you seek out an OB/GYN or midwife, don't hesitate to interview multiple clinicians before you settle on someone to care for you in your pregnancy. As in all medical fields, some clinicians are more tuned into mental health concerns than others. If they are, they're probably keeping up to date on the latest medical guidelines for treatment of anxiety, depression, and other psychiatric concerns. Some questions to ask are:

» What experience do you have with mental health care?

» How frequently do you see patients who have had depression and anxiety related to pregnancy or postpartum?

» How do you approach treating depression and anxiety? Are you familiar with the current research on treatment options and prescribing medication during pregnancy and lactation?

» Do you have a list of mental health professionals you refer to? Do these clinicians specialize in treating depression and anxiety in pregnancy and postpartum?

Some clinicians may be less oriented toward mental health care. They may be experts in other aspects of pregnancy, which may or may not apply to you. It might take a few tries to find the obstetrician or midwife that is the right fit. If you have a therapist or psychiatrist, ask them if they know of specific medical clinicians and can offer recommendations as you build your care team. If you have open lines of communication with other parents who have struggled, they may be a resource for recommendations as well.

All of the above also applies to finding a pediatrician to care for your child. You may find that, even though mom or dad is not their patient, a pediatrician may screen new parents for postpartum depression and anxiety symptoms, using the EPDS or another tool. While they probably won't treat these concerns themselves, it's helpful to have a pediatrician who is comfortable talking about these topics and who has a good referral network, should a parent need it. As above, asking your psychiatrist or therapist or other parents who've struggled with mental health concerns for recommendations can steer you in a useful direction.

Thinking about the past and planning for the future will be enormously helpful as you aim to improve on your experience with future pregnancies and reduce the risk of recurrent postpartum depression or anxiety symptoms. Read on to Chapter 14 to make a specific plan for your future postpartum experience.

CHAPTER 14

YOUR POSTPARTUM PLAN

At some point during prenatal appointments, your medical clinician may introduce the idea of a *birth plan*. A birth plan helps expectant parents think through various aspects of labor and delivery *before* the process starts. You'll be asked to consider things like where and how you'd like to labor in the early stages, who will be in the delivery room, and what kind of pain management strategies you'd like to use. This is a useful exercise because it helps you anticipate various scenarios and prepare for them to some degree. We encourage future parents to be flexible in formulating a birth plan and about how they envision their birth happening; babies come into the world in hundreds of different ways. Women who have highly specific expectations often feel disappointed that their birth didn't go exactly how they hoped. However, having a general outline of expectations and desires can be valuable in easing some of the anxiety associated with labor and delivery.

In the same way that birth plans can be helpful, a *postpartum plan* is also useful, but rarely do people take the time to think about one. It can be particularly difficult to anticipate and plan if it's your first child because no matter how many books or blogs or parenting articles you read ahead of time, no one can truly predict what their experience will be until they actually live through it.

We developed this worksheet, My Postpartum Plan, after speaking with hundreds of new parents about their struggles after bringing home a new baby. As with a birth plan, we encourage you to do this exercise *before* the baby arrives. People often find that their expectations for what things will be like are different from what their partner or other support people envision. It's far more helpful and much less stressful to discover these differences ahead of time, rather than at 2:00 am, when the baby is crying.

Here's how we suggest you fill out this worksheet. The first column lists areas of potential concern that may arise postpartum. The pregnant person completes the second column

(Ideas for Myself) with their expectations for how the given topic will be addressed or accomplished. Then, their partner/support person fills in their responses and expectations in the third column (Ideas for My Partner/Support People). After that, we suggest you sit down together to discuss your answers. Where are the similarities? The differences? Were there answers that surprised either of you? After this discussion, you may need to modify your answers (along with your expectations) and renegotiate your strategies to manage these issues. Last, start working on the fourth column (Plan to Make it Happen). This column should include strategies to meet the needs of both people.

My Postpartum Plan

Topic	Ideas for Myself	Ideas for My Partner/ Support People	Plan to Make it Happen
Nighttime help/duties			
Daytime help/duties			
Asking for help			
Feeding/ breast- feeding			
Basic needs/ hygiene			
Mental and emotional health			

Visitors			
Caring for older children			
Time for yourself			
Time with your partner/ date nights			
Intimacy			
Exercise or movement (once cleared by your doctor)			
Nutrition			

The fourth column in this worksheet should be a living document. We encourage people to fill it in with what you *think* will work. Then, once your new baby is home, revisit this worksheet and see if you're keeping up with the plan. If you are, great! Is it helping? If you're not doing the things in the last column, why not? Has it slipped your mind? Did you try it, and the strategy didn't work? Are you doing something you expected but in a different way than you first planned? It's important to reevaluate your plan and make adjustments as needed in those first weeks and beyond. Babies and their needs change so much in the first year of life that you have to remain flexible to get your needs met, your partner's needs met, and keep up with daily tasks like housework, getting to work, and having social time.

A great way to fill in the fourth column is to ask other experienced parents what has worked for them when they had a new baby at home? You can also revisit the previous chapters in this book; each chapter's PARENTS method section will give you ideas. Stay flexible as you brainstorm options. You may need to modify suggestions or ideas that you see in this book or get from other people, but talking with others who've been through this means that you don't always need to start from square one.

On the next page is an example of a post-partum plan for a couple that is having their second child. Many of their answers also apply to first-time or multiple-time parents. They've had a newborn before, so they have some idea what to expect, but lots can change from the first to the second child. Work demands may be different. Support people who could help the first time may not be available this time around. Even though you've cared for a new-born before, you haven't had a newborn *and* an older child at home, so whether this is your first child, second, third, or beyond, take time to think about your expectations.

Sample - My Postpartum Plan

Topic	Ideas for Myself	Ideas for My Partner/ Support People	Plan to Make it Happen
Nighttime help/duties	I'll do most but will need help	She'll do nighttime because I have to go to work in the morning	
Daytime help/duties	I will do everything	My mom would like to come over to help	
Asking for help	I think I can do it; I'll ask for help when I need it	She'll be fine; I hope she'll ask if she needs help	
Feeding/ breast- feeding	My goal is to breastfeed for a year	I'm okay with whatever she wants to do	
Basic needs/ hygiene	I'd like to shower at least every other day	I don't have any concerns with this	

Mental and emotional health	Given how I felt after my first, I think I will struggle with feeling overwhelmed	I'm worried about how we'll manage taking care of 2 kids. When I get stressed, I tend to get frustrated, and I don't want that to happen	
Visitors	I'd like to limit visitors for the first 2 weeks	My parents want to come to the hospital right away and will stay at our house for a week	
Caring for older children	I'd like to pull our toddler out of daycare to save money while I'm on maternity leave	Since she's home, she'll be responsible for both kids	
Time for yourself	I'd like this, but don't expect it when the baby is little	I'd like to still go to the gym 3x a week and stay in my basketball league	

Time with your partner/ date night	A date night once a month	A date night every 2 weeks	
Intimacy	I'd like this to happen, but I know it will be hard to find time and the energy	I'd still like to have sex twice a week	
Exercise or movement (once cleared by your doctor)	I'd like to be able to work out 2–3x/ week	I go to the gym 3x a week, and I play basketball	
Nutrition	I haven't yet, but I should make some meals to have in the freezer	I can help cook, or we can order food	

There are usually a few areas on this worksheet that generate the most conflict. They are: nighttime duties, visitors, intimacy, time for yourself, and caring for older children. In these areas, expectations are often different for each parent, and conflict can arise because they aren't communicating well about these differences. It's worthwhile to be particularly thoughtful about these 5 areas and to have honest conversations about possible solutions. This can be especially important if you struggled with these areas after your previous child/children were born. Think back to how things played out before, and if you feel things didn't go well, take time to brainstorm alternative strategies to address those conflicts. If you're struggling to do this on your own, a few sessions with a couple's therapist can be a great option.

You may have noticed a recurring theme in this chapter: *flexibility*. Babies and children change so much and can be unpredictable; being flexible helps you stay resilient and avoid overly rigid expectations of yourself and your partner. Remember, your baby is learning how to be a baby, and you're practicing being a parent. It's okay to be on the learning curve together.

CHAPTER 15

SELECTED RESOURCES

There are many resources available to new parents, and new ones are always arriving on the scene, so it would be impossible to list them all here. Below are some we frequently recommend for our patients, although we are not directly affiliated with the organizations below. You can also check with your healthcare clinicians about local resources in your area.

Maternal and Parental Mental Health

Postpartum Support International (PSI)

» www.postpartum.net

» PSI has information for moms and for dads, including a HelpLine (English and Spanish) to assist parents in getting connected to mental health professionals in

their geographic area who have experience treating perinatal mood and anxiety
disorders.

» They also offer weekly and monthly online
support groups and chats in which new
parents can talk to and ask questions of
an expert.

National Suicide Prevention Hotline
1-800-273-TALK (8255)

Massachusetts General Hospital Center for Women's Mental Health

» www.womensmentalhealth.org

» This site contains a wealth of information
about maternal mental health. In particular,
there is well-researched, evidence-based
information about the use of medications
in pregnancy and breastfeeding

2020MOM

» www.2020MOM.org

» 2020MOM is an organization working to
close gaps in maternal mental healthcare

delivery, provide education about PMADs, and work for policy change to improve health care for families.

Peer Groups for Moms

In-Person Groups

- » www.meetup.com (4,000+ groups for parents)

- » www.mochamoms.org (for mothers of color, with over 100 local chapters)

- » www.mops.org (for mothers of preschoolers)

- » www.multiplesofamerica.org (for moms of multiples)

- » www.momsclub.com (for at-home moms)

Online Communities/Resources

- » www.circleofmoms.com

- » www.cafemom.com

- » www.workingmomkind.com (for moms who work other jobs in addition to parenting)

- » https://lauravanderkam.com/podcast/

- » www.momenough.com (podcast covering a variety of parenting topics)

Lactation Support

Online Support

- » Breastfeed Inc. - www.breastfeedinc.com

- » La Leche League International - www.LLLI.org

- » KellyMom - www.kellymom.com

In-Person

- » Many birth centers and hospitals have lactation consultants on staff.

- » For drop-in lactation support, BabyCafeUSA - www.babycafeUSA.org

- » Women, Infants, and Children (WIC) peer counseling program. WIC offers breast-feeding support for WIC-eligible women.

- » Lactation consultants in private practice may offer the option of coming to your home. To find a Lactation Consultant, visit

these sites, which have lactation consultants listed by their geographical area.

» International Lactation Consultant
Association - www.ILCA.org

» United States Lactation Consultant
Association - www.USLCA.org

Other Resources

Erikson Fussy Baby Network

» www.erikson.edu/fussy-baby-network

» The Erikson Fussy Baby Network offers
phone consultations in English and Spanish
with infant specialists for helping families
struggling with an infant's sleeping, crying,
or feeding.

Phone/Tablet Apps

There are many useful, good-quality apps out there for moms/dads/parents. Because the options are so varied and new apps are created so often, we recommend talking with clinicians, support people, and/or finding recommendations online. We recommend looking into apps in these general areas:

» For tracking baby's physical and cognitive development and milestones

» For tracking the baby's sleep, feedings, wet diapers, etc.

» For music: lullaby playlists, soothing playlists for parents' sleep, or just to have in the background

» For relaxation and meditation

References

Abramowitz, J.S., Melter-Brody, S., Leserman, J., Killenberg, S., Rinaldi, K., Mahaffey, B.L., & Peterson, C. (2010). Obsessional thoughts and compulsive behaviors in a sample of women with postpartum mood symptoms. *Archive of Women's Mental Health, 13*(6), 523-530.

American Psychiatric Association. (2013). *Diagnostic and statistical manual of mental disorders* (5th ed.), Author. Retrieved from https://doi.org/10.1176/appi.books.9780890425596

Beaudoin, L. P. (2014). *The possibility of super-somnolent mentation: A new information-processing approach to sleep-onset acceleration and insomnia exemplified by serial diverse imagining.* Retrieved from http://summit.sfu.ca/item/12143

Beck, C.T. (2004). Birth trauma: In the eye of the beholder. *Nursing Research, 53*(1), 28-35.

Beck, C.T., Driscoll, J.W., & Watson, S. (2013) *Traumatic childbirth.* Routledge.

Cohen, L.S., Altshuler, L.L., Harlow, B.L., Nonacs, R., Newport, D. J., Viguera, A. C., Suri, R., Burt, V.K., Hendrick, V., Reminick, A.M., Loughead, A., Vitonis, A.F., & Stowe, Z.N. (2006). Relapse of major depression during pregnancy in women who maintain or discontinue antidepressant treatment. *JAMA, 295*(5), 499-507.

Cox, J.L., & Sagovsky, R. (1987). Detection of postnatal depression: Development of the 10-item Edinburgh Postnatal Depression Scale. *British Journal of Psychiatry, 150,* 782-786.

Etheridge, J., & Slade, P. (2017). "Nothing's actually happened to me.": The experiences of fathers who found childbirth traumatic. *BMC Pregnancy and Childbirth, 17,* 80.

Fairbrother, N., & Woody, S.R. (2008). New mothers' thoughts of harm related to the newborn. *Archives of Women's Mental Health, 11,* 221-229.

Glynn, L.M., & Sandman, C.A. (2011). Prenatal Origins of Neurological Development: A critical period for fetus and mother. *Current Directions in Psychological Science, 20(6),* 384-389.

Hales, T. (2021). *Hale's Medications and Mothers' Milk.* Springer Publishing.

Hoekzema, E., Barba-Müller, E., Pozzobon, C., Picado, M., Lucco, F., García-García, D., Soliva, J.C., Tobeña, A., Desco, M., Crone, E.A., Ballesteros, A., Carmona, S., & Vilarroya, O. (2017). Pregnancy leads to long-lasting changes in human brain structure. *Nature Neuroscience, 20,* 287–296.

Howell, E.A., Mora, P.A., Horowitz, C.R. & Leventhal, H. (2005). Racial and ethnic differences in factors associated with early postpartum depressive symptoms. *Obstetrics and Gynecology, 105(6),* 1442-1450.

Linehan, M.M. (2014). *DBT skills training manual.* The Guilford Press.

Kozhimannil, K.B, Trinacty, C.M., Busch, A.B., Huskamp, H.A., & Adams, A.S. (2011). Racial and ethnic disparities in postpartum depression care among low-income women. *Psychiatric Services, 62(6),* 619–625.

Mayo Clinic. (2021). *Depression and anxiety: Exercise eases symptoms.* Retrieved from https://www.mayoclinic.org/diseases-conditions/depression/in-depth/depression-and-exercise/art-20046495

Massachusetts General Hospital Center for Women's Mental Health. (2021). *Postpartum psychiatric disorders.* Retrieved from https://womensmentalhealth.org/specialty-clinics/postpartum-psychiatric-disorders/

Netz, Yael. (2017). Is the Comparison between Exercise and Pharmacologic Treatment of Depression in the Clinical Practice Guideline of the American College of Physicians Evidence-Based? *Frontiers in Pharmacology, 8,* 257.

Norcross, J.C., & Wampold, B.E. (Eds.). (2019). *Psychotherapy relationships that work: Volume 2: Evidence-based therapist responsiveness (3 Ed).* Oxford University Press.

Paulson, J.F., & Bazemore, S.D. (2010). *Prenatal and postpartum depression in fathers and its association with maternal depression: A meta-analysis.* JAMA, 303(19), 1961–1969.

Postpartum Support International. (2021). *Depression during pregnancy & postpartum.* Retrieved from https://www.postpartum.net/learn-more/depression/

Postpartum Support International. (2021). *Pregnancy or postpartum obsessive symptoms.* Retrieved from https://www.postpartum.net/learn-more/obsessive-symptoms/

Postpartum Support International. (2021). *Postpartum mental health is a men's issue.* Retrieved from https://www.postpartum.net/get-help/help-for-dads/

Postpartum Support International. (2021). *Postpartum posttraumatic stress disorder.* Retrieved from https://www.postpartum.net/learn-more/postpartum-post-traumatic-stress-disorder/

Watson, N. M., Safwan Badr, M., Belenky, G., Bliwise, D.L., Buxton, O.M., Buysse, D., et al. (2015). Recommended amount of sleep for a healthy adult: A joint consensus statement of the American Academy of Sleep Medicine and Sleep Research Society. *Sleep, 38*(6), 843-844.

Samuelson, K.W. (2011). Post-traumatic stress disorder and declarative memory functioning: A review. *Dialogues in Clinical Neuroscience, 13(3)*, 346-351.

Simpson, M. and Catling, C. (2015). Understanding psychological traumatic birth experiences: A literature review. *Women and Birth, 19 (2016)*, 203-207.

Wenzel, A., Gorman, L., O'Hara, M., & Stuart, S. (2001). The occurrence of panic and obsessive-compulsive symptoms in women with postpartum dysphoria: Prospective study. *Archives of Women's Mental Health, 4*(1), 5–12.

Wenzel, A., Haugen, E.N., Jackson, L.C., & Brendle, J.R. (2005). Anxiety symptoms and disorders at eight weeks postpartum. *Journal of Anxiety Disorders, 19*(3), 295311.

Research on the Safety of Psychiatric Medications During Pregnancy and Lactation

There are hundreds of studies related to the safety of psychiatric medications in pregnancy and lactation, and more are always being published. We include a selection of such studies below.

Bandoli, G., Chambers, C.D., Wells, A., & Palmsten, K. (2020). Perinatal antidepressant use and risk of adverse neonatal outcomes. *Pediatrics, 146*(1):e20192493.

Casper, R.C., Fleisher, C.E., Lee-Ancajas, J.C., Gilles, A., Gaylor, E., DeBattista, A., & Hoyme, H.E. (2003). Follow-up of children of depressed mothers exposed or not exposed to antidepressant drugs during pregnancy. *Journal of Pediatrics, 142*(4), 402-408.

Cohen, L.S., & Nonacs, R. (2016). Neurodevelopmental implications of fetal exposure to selective serotonin reuptake inhibitors and untreated maternal depression. *JAMA Psychiatry, 73*(11), 1170-1172.

Cohen, L.S. (2017). Evolving practice in perinatal psychiatry: Lessons learned. *OB/GYN News.* Retrieved from https://womensmentalhealth.org/obgyn/evolving-practice-perinatal-psychopharmacology-lessons-learned/

Flores, J.M., Avila-Quintero, V.J., & Bloch, M.H. (2019). Selective serotonin reuptake inhibitor use during pregnancy: Associated with but not causative of autism in offspring. *JAMA Psychiatry, 76*(12), 1225-1227.

Freeman, M.P., Goez-Mogollon, L., McInerney, K.A., Davies, A.C., Church, T.R., Sosinsky, A.Z. et al. (2018). Obstetrical and neonatal outcomes after benzodiazepine exposure during pregnancy. *General Hospital Psychiatry, 53,* 73-79.

Larsen, E.R., Damkier, P., Pederson, L.H., Fenger-Gron, J., Mikkelsen, R.L., Nielsen, R.E., et al.. (2015). Use of psychotropic drugs during pregnancy and breast-feeding. *Acta Psychiatrica Scandinavica Supplementum, 445,* 1-28.

Lupatelli, A., Wood, M., Ystrom, E., Skurtveit, S., Handal, M., & Nordeng, H. (2017). Effect of time-dependent selective serotonin reuptake inhibitor antidepressants during pregnancy in behavioral, emotional, and social development in preschool-age children. *Journal of the AACAP, 57*(3), 200-208.

McElhatton, P.R. (1994). The effects of benzodiazepine use during pregnancy and lactation. *Reproductive Toxicology, 8*(6), 461-475.

Moses-Kolko, E.L., Bogen, D., Perel, J., Bregar, A., Uhl, K., Levin, B., & Wisner, K.L. (2005). Neonatal signs after late in utero exposure to serotonin reuptake inhibitors: Literature review and implications for clinical applications. *American Journal of Psychiatry, 293*(19), 2372-2383.

Nulman, I., Koren, G., Rovet, J., Barrera, M., Pulver, A., Streiner, D., & Feldman, B. (2012). Neurodevelopment of children following prenatal exposure to venlafaxine, selective- serotonin reuptake inhibitors, or untreated maternal depression. *American Journal of Psychiatry, 169*(11), 1165-1174.

Oberlander, T.F., Warburton, W., Misri, S., Aghajanian, J., & Hertzman, C. (2006). Neonatal outcomes after prenatal exposure to selective serotonin reuptake inhibitor antidepressants and maternal depression using population-based linked health data. *Archives of General Psychiatry, 63*(8), 898-906.

Rommel, A.S., Bergink, V., Liu, X., Munk-Olsen, T., & Molenaar, N.M. (2020). Long-term effects of intra-uterine exposure to antidepressants on physical, neurodevelopmental, and psychiatric outcomes: A systematic review. *Journal of Clinical Psychiatry, 81*(3):19r12965.

Ross, L.E., Grigoriadis, S., & Mamisashvili, L. (2013). Selected pregnancy and delivery outcomes after exposure to antidepressant medication: A systematic review and meta-analysis. *JAMA Psychiatry, 70*(4), 436-443.

Sujan, A.C., Oberg, A.S., Quinn, P.D., & D'Onofrio, B.M. (2018). Annual research review: Maternal anti-depressant use during pregnancy and offspring neurodevelopmental problems. *Journal of Child Psychology and Psychiatry, 60*(4), 356-376.

Warburton, W., Hertzman, C., & Oberlander, T.F. (2010). A register study of the impact of stopping third tri-mester selective serotonin reuptake inhibitor exposure on neonatal health. *Acta Psychiatrica Scandinavica, 121*(6), 471-479.

Wilson, K.L., Zelig, C.M., Harvey, J.P., Cunningham, B.S., Dolinsky, B.M., & Napolitano, P.G. (2011). Persistent pulmonary hypertension of the newborn is associated with mode of delivery and not with maternal use of selective serotonin reuptake inhibitors. *American Journal of Perinatology, 28*(1), 19-24.

Wisner, K.L., Gelenberg, A.J., Leonard, H., Zarin, D., & Frank, E. (1999). Pharmacologic treatment of depression during pregnancy. *JAMA, 282*(13): 1264-1269.

Wisner, K.L., Sit, D.K.Y., Hanusa, B.H., Moses-Kolko, E.L., Bogen, D.L., Hunker, D.F., et al. (2009). Major depression and antidepressant treatment: Impact on pregnancy and neonatal outcomes. *American Journal of Psychiatry, 166*(5), 557-566.

ABOUT THE AUTHORS

Gabrielle Mauren, PhD is a psychologist and developer of an award-winning reproductive mental health program. She did her undergraduate studies, graduate studies, and postgraduate fellowship at the University of Iowa, the University of Minnesota, and the University of Pennsylvania, respectively. She has been a featured speaker at local, national, and international conferences, and a contributor to articles on the topic of perinatal mental health. She lives in Minnesota with her husband and daughter.

Michelle Wiersgalla, MD is a reproductive psychiatrist and psychopharmacology consultant. She attended college and medical school at the University of Wisconsin and did her psychiatry residency at the Harvard Longwood Program. Michelle has repeatedly been recognized as a Top Doctor in psychiatry. She has been a featured speaker at local and national conferences on the topics of perinatal mental health and psychopharmacological approaches to treatment. She lives in Minnesota with her husband and two daughters.

Made in the USA
Middletown, DE
10 May 2024